Maps of Water & Hope:

Selected Works

Susan D. Baker

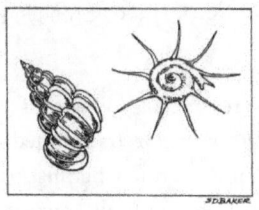

N. V. Baker, editor
Nightwatchman Press LLC
New Mexico

Cover artwork by Susan D. Baker
Cover & interior design by CreateSpace & N. V. Baker

DEDICATION

To Daniel Garcia, a true friend

CONTENTS

POEMS

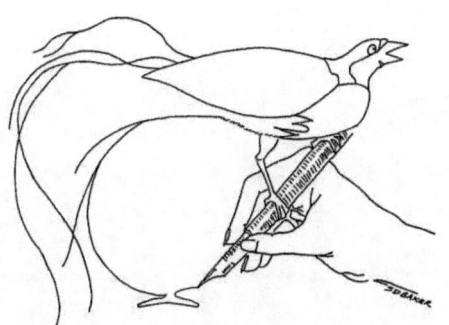

EDITOR'S NOTE

My sister Susan D. Baker worked for years as a poet, novelist and artist, largely self-taught. Place always informed her work: from her childhood in Texas to coming of age in southern California and San Francisco, from artistic pursuits in the South Pacific to exploring New Orleans and the Gulf Coast. For almost twenty years, following her diagnosis with multiple sclerosis, she has lived in Tucson.

Ravaging illness has gradually robbed her of the ability to draw, to write, to travel and sometimes even to speak. I hope that, to a small degree, this book may speak for her. As for me, I heard her voice constantly as the manuscript took shape.

The drawings, poems and short story I have included here – with contributions from our other sister Barbara Baker and friend Debra Denker - highlight Susan's exceptional and varied creativity. Throughout, except in a few obvious cases of typographical errors, I have followed her decisions and vision. On a few occasions, I have provided parenthetical notes to assist the reader.

In addition to Barbara and Debra, thanks are due to Jim Graham for technical assistance scanning in the drawings. For their ongoing care of Susan, much gratitude to the people at Foothills Rehab Center in Tucson and Soreo Hospice.

This book is dedicated to Danny Garcia, for being a kind, funny and generous-hearted friend to Susan for many years, and to the entire family.

Intended both to honor Susan's life's work and delight readers, this book also illustrates the heavy toll of multiple sclerosis, a terrible disease that took our father's life as well.

All profits from the sale of this book go to the National Multiple Sclerosis Society for research to "end MS forever." For more information, or to donate directly, visit
https://www.nationalmssociety.org/

N. V. Baker
Las Cruces, New Mexico
January 2018

MAP 1
NEW YORKER DREAMS

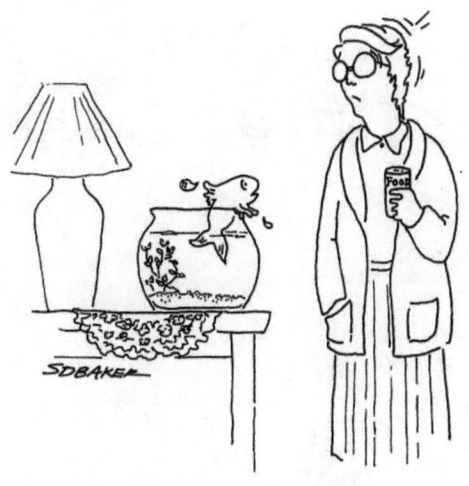

"You'd tell me if I was adopted, wouldn't you?"

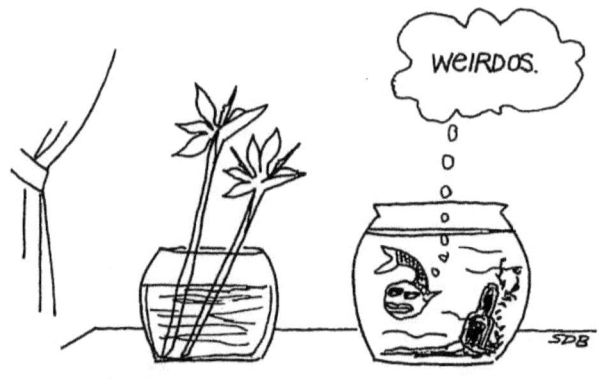

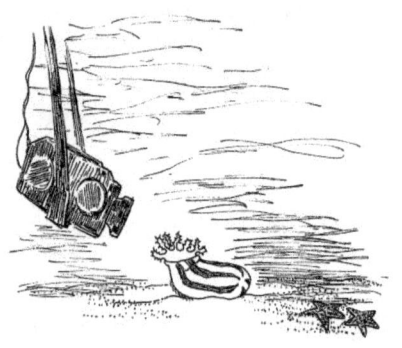

So what am I supposed to do, tap dance?

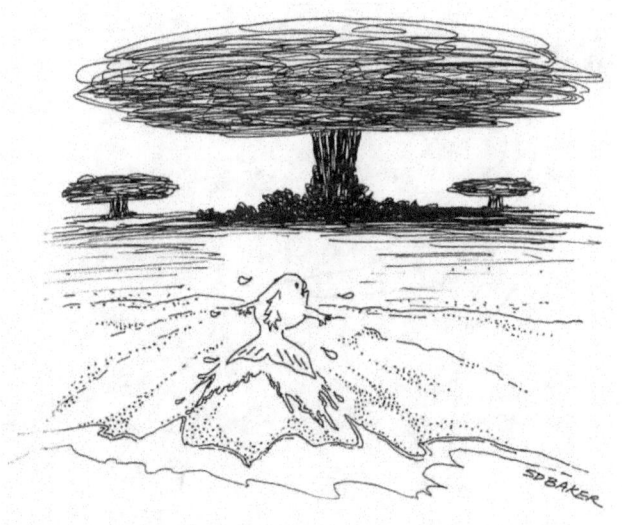

Drat! Just as I learned to walk!

You Know You're a Cat Lover If ...

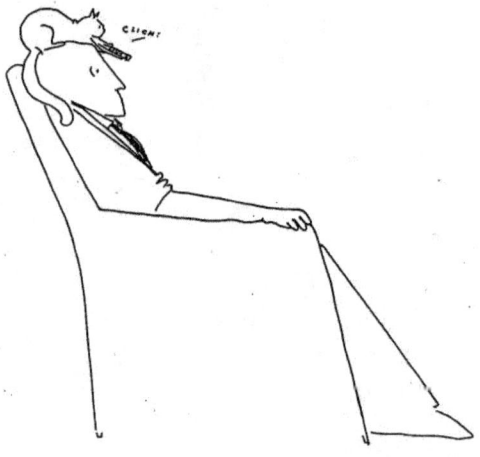

you watch what your cat wants to watch.

You Know You're a Cat Lover If ...

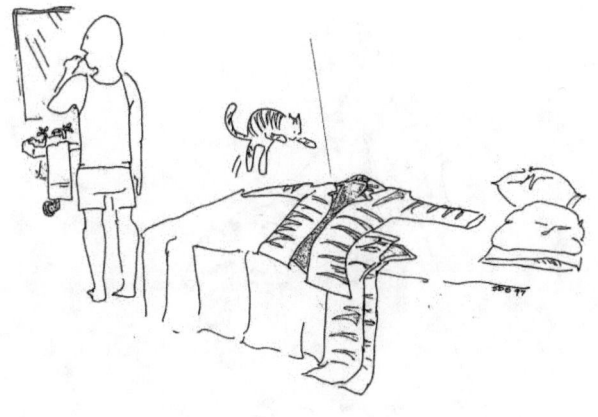

you buy your clothes to match your cat.

You Know You're a Cat Lover If ....

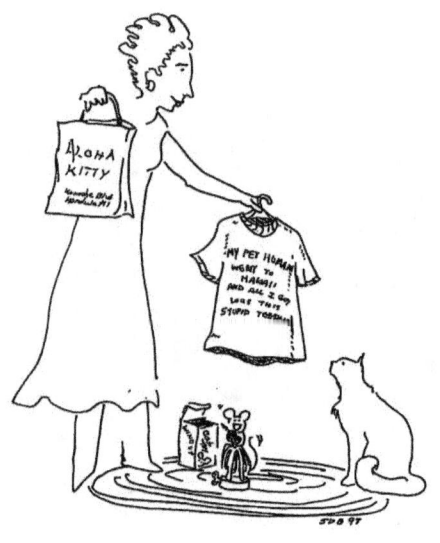

... you go on vacation and buy gifts for your cat.

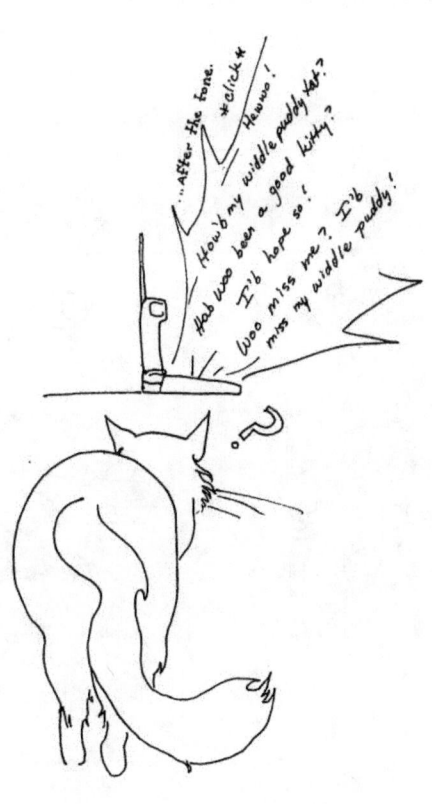

7

Socks dreams of New Orleans…

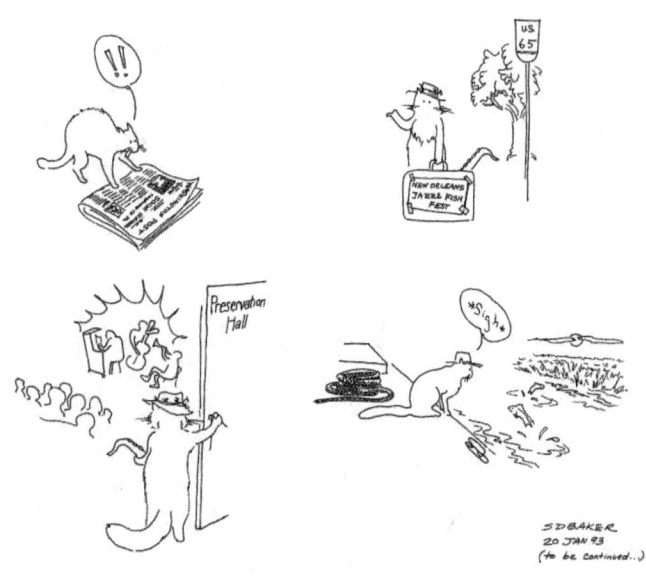

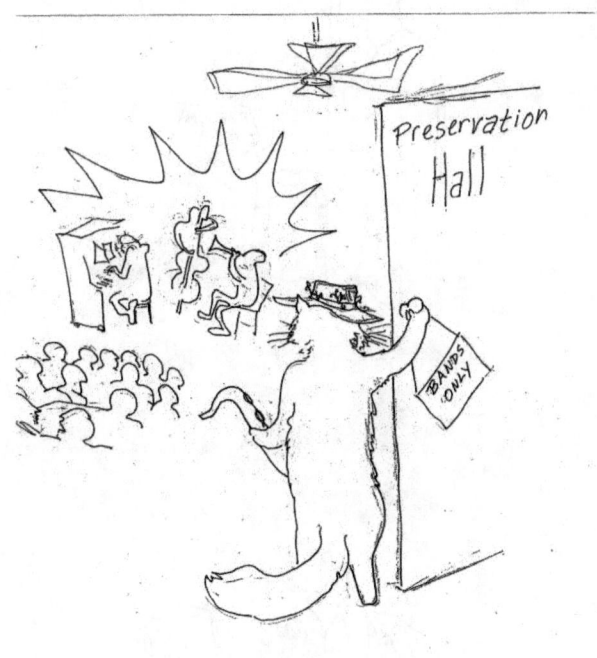

Kitty Beausoleil (aka Socks) at his debut

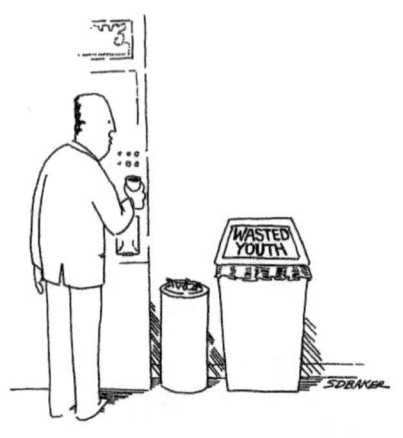

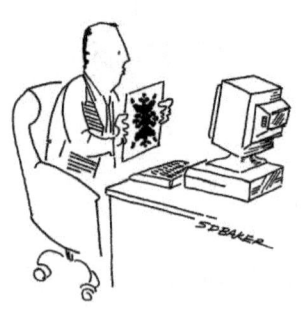

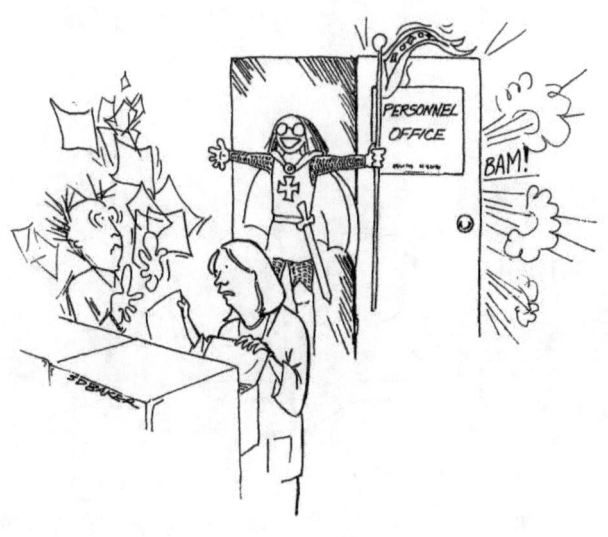

"Recent graduate."

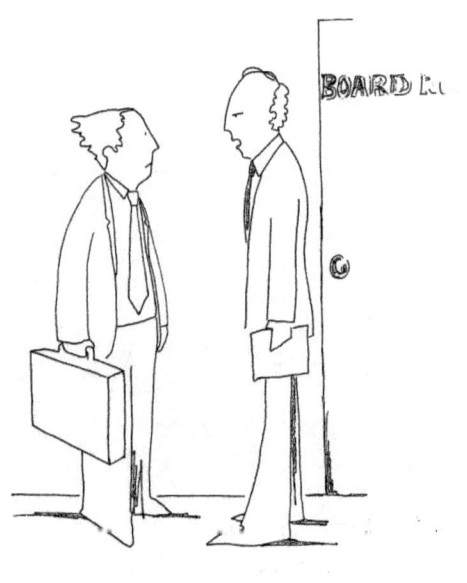

"Frankly, Simmons, your idea is inane, your presentation boring, your facts absurd, and your credentials for the birds. But, say, I like that tie you're wearing."

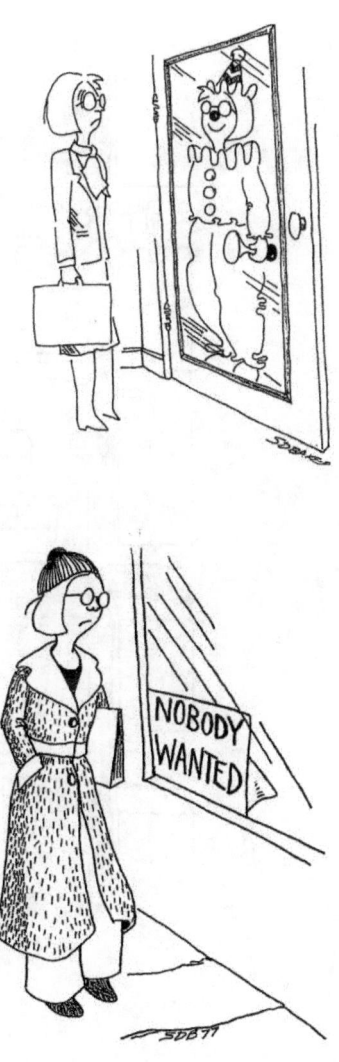

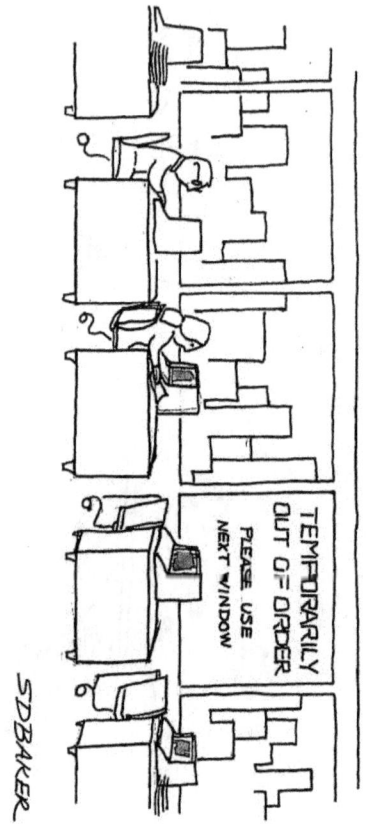

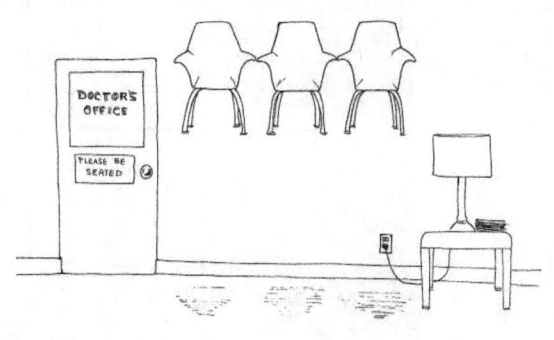

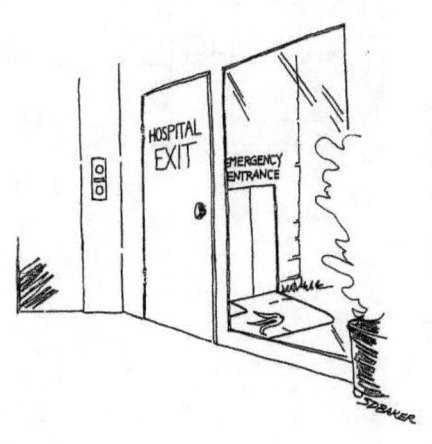

15

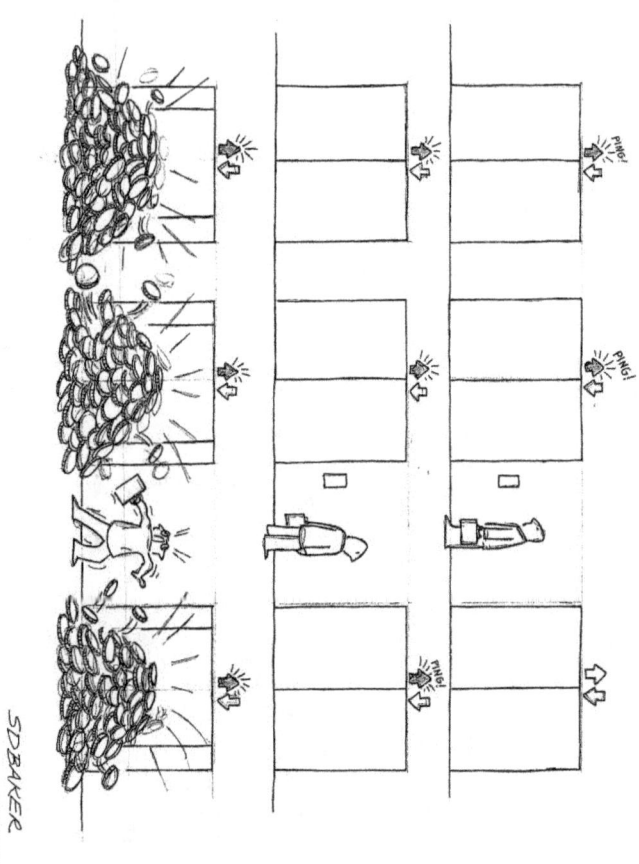

SDBAKER

16

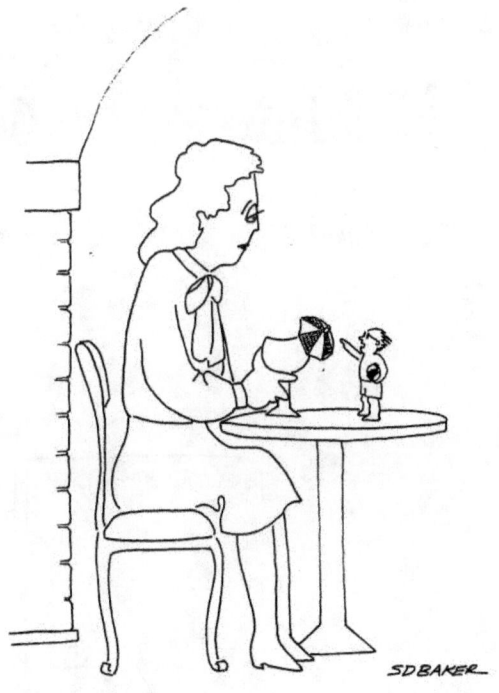

"Hey, lady! That's my umbrella!"

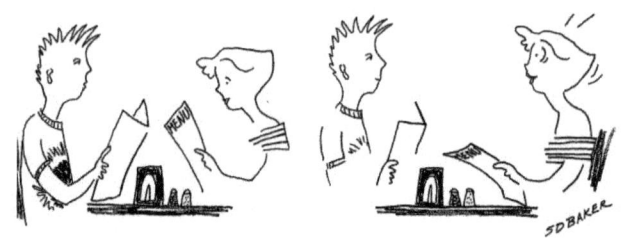

"Let's go dutch."   *"You mean you've got money?!"*

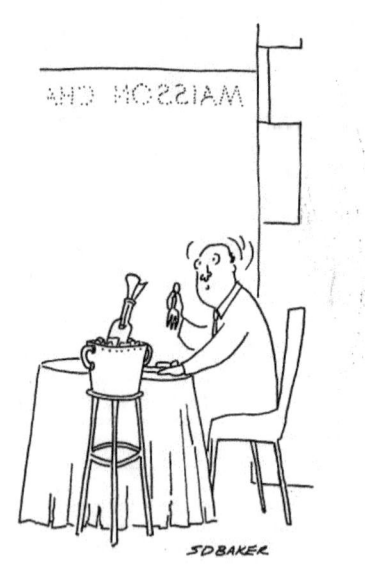

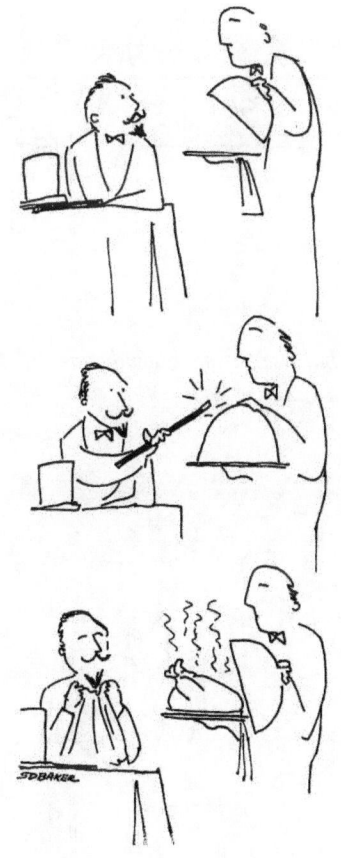

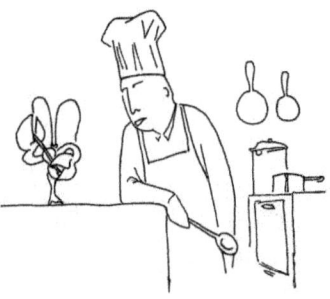

"What else do you know besides 'Copacabana'?"

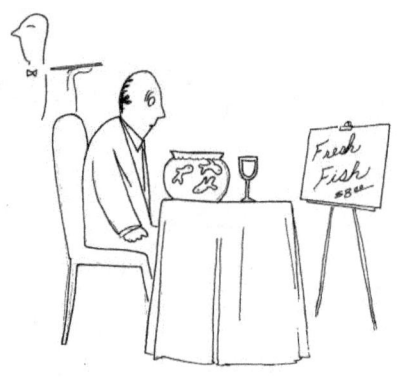

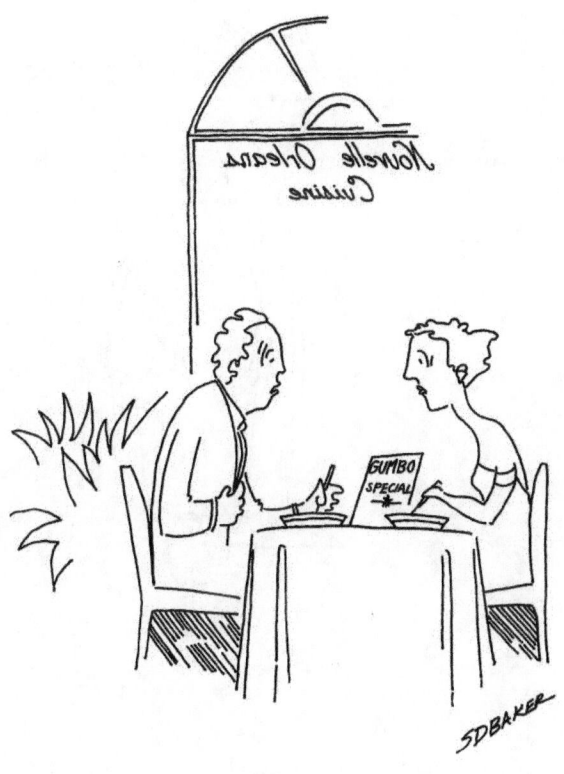

"I'm sure I saw this die on National Geographic."

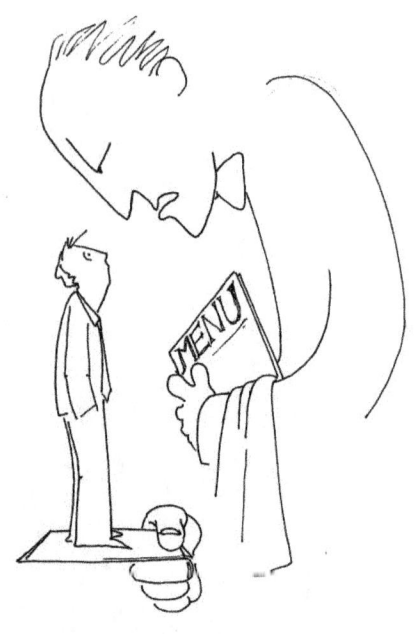

"*What do you MEAN, she left you for a tip?*"

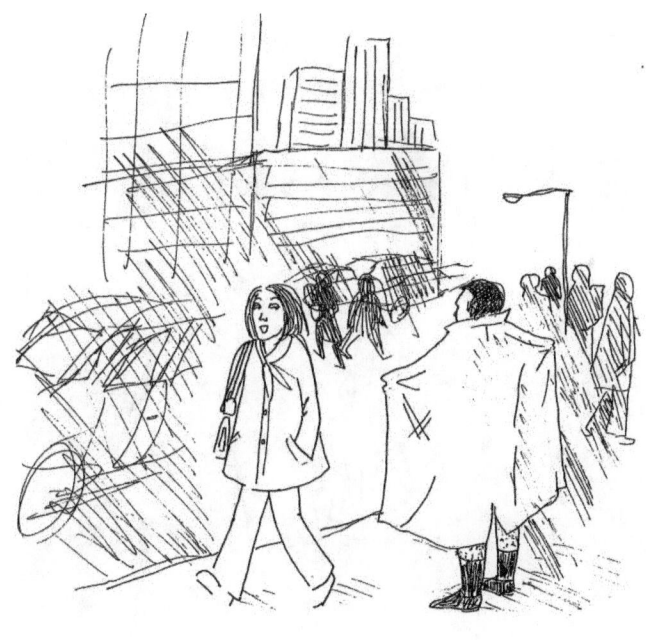

"Congratulations. I see you passed your taxidermy class."

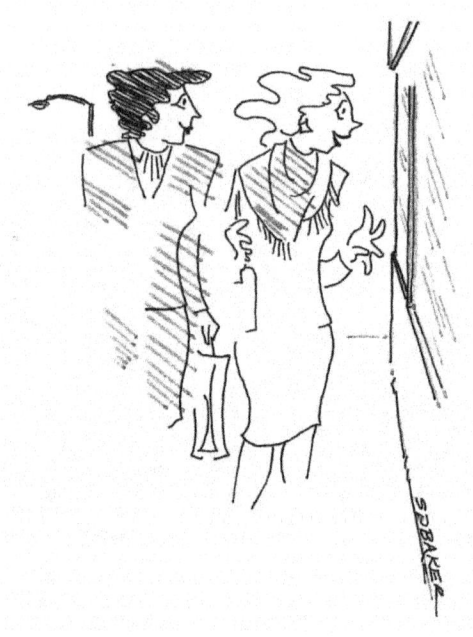

"Oh, look – An antique Cuisinart!"

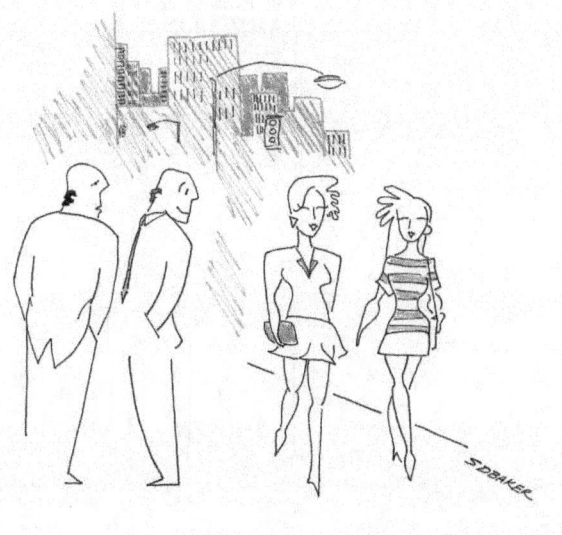

"Yeah, miniskirts. But the next thing you know, hair's back."

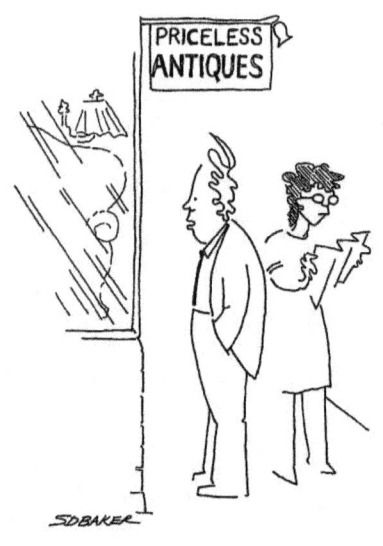

"*Remember that old dead owl I found in the barn a few years back? Well, lookee here…*"

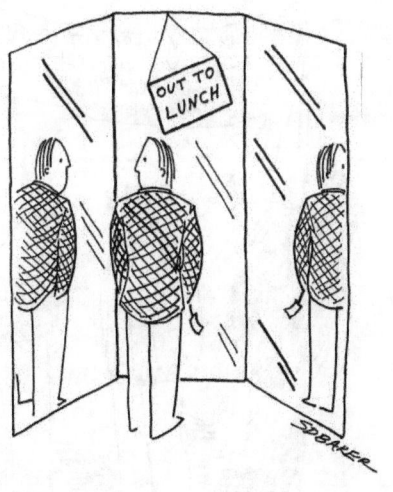

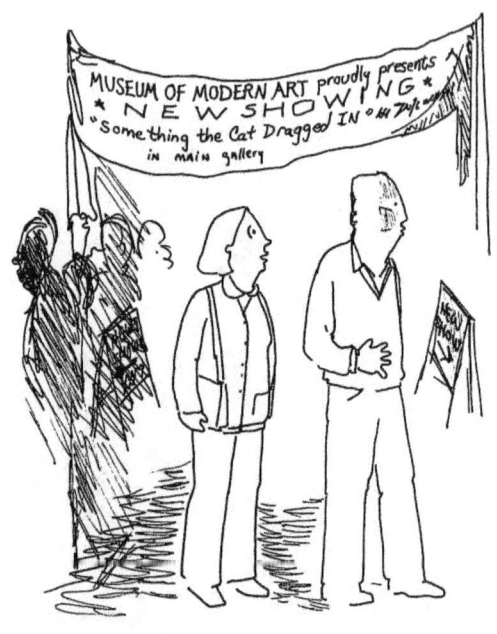

"Look at it this way, dear. At least Realism's back."

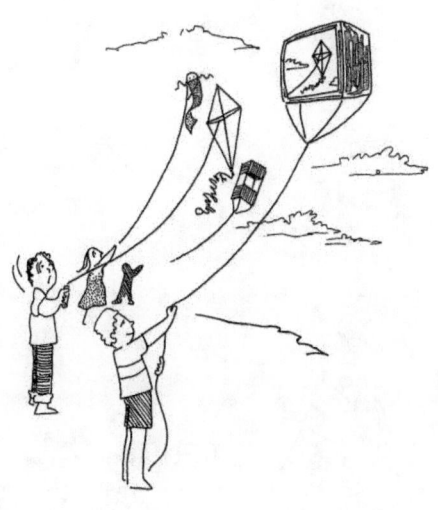

Strategic & Cultural CONTRIBUTIONS
         of the ancient TRILOBITES:

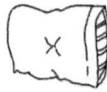

Fig. 1A: instrument of war

Fig. 1B: instrument of peace

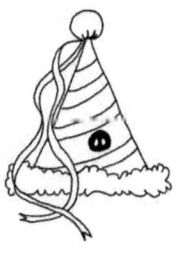

Fig. 1C: rudimentary shelter;
         conceptual origin of the
         calcareous shell (note also
         the uncanny resemblance to
         a modern-day party hat).

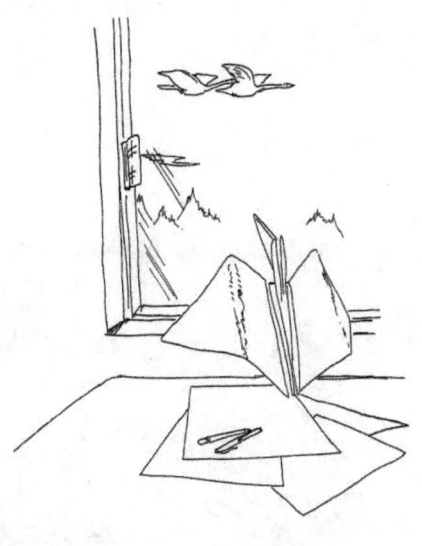

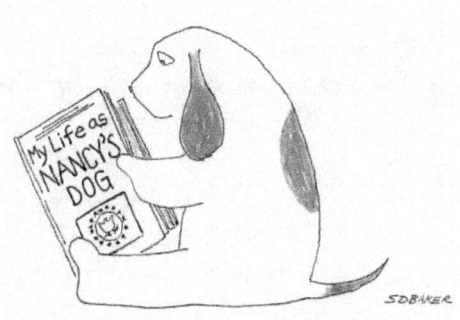

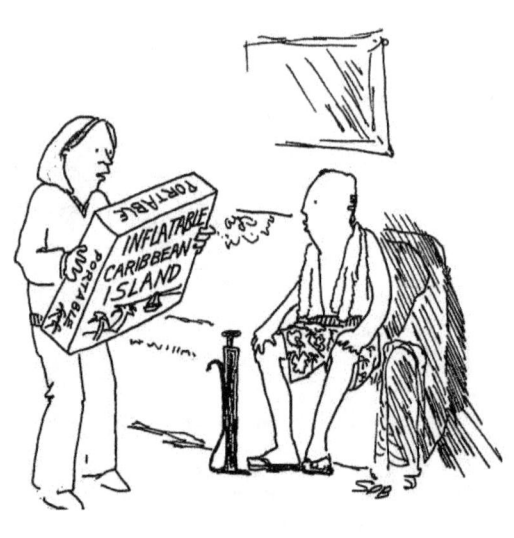

"I hate to disappoint you, dear, but I think it's just one of those time-share scams."

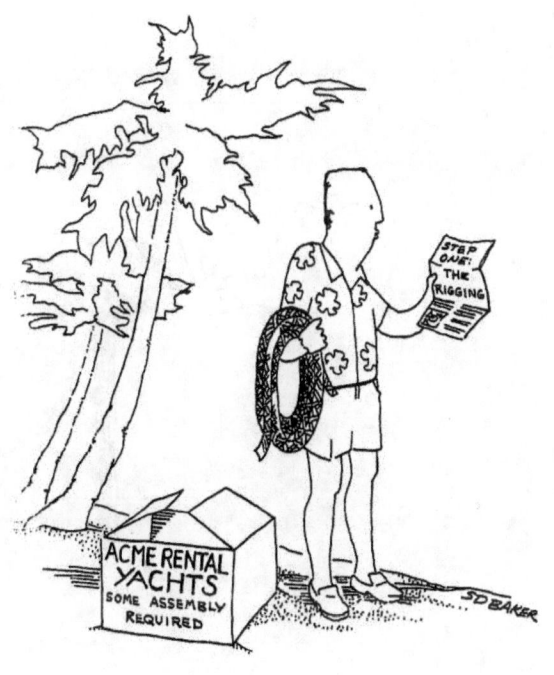

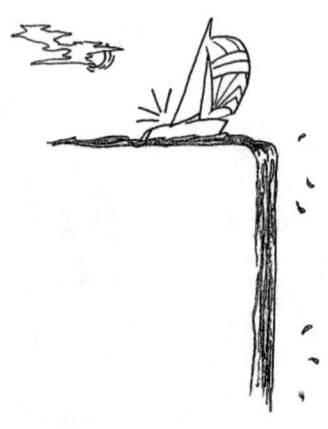

"You sure you got the hang of the Loran-C?"

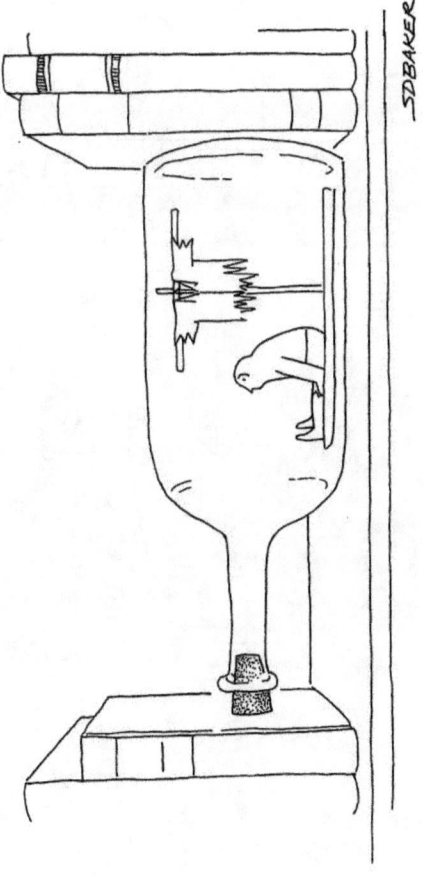

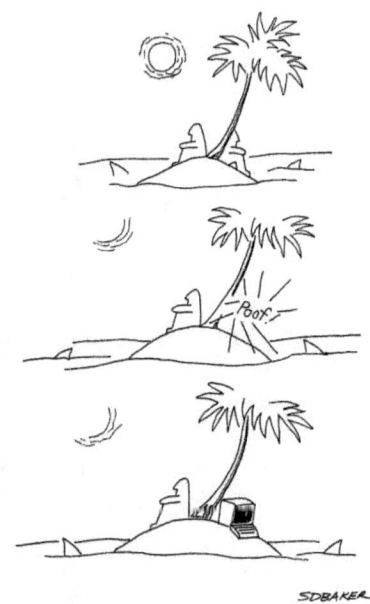

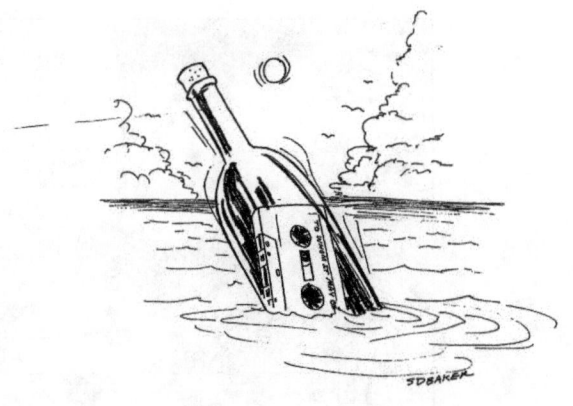

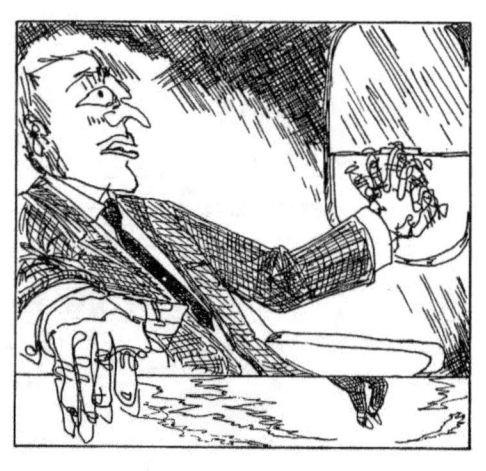

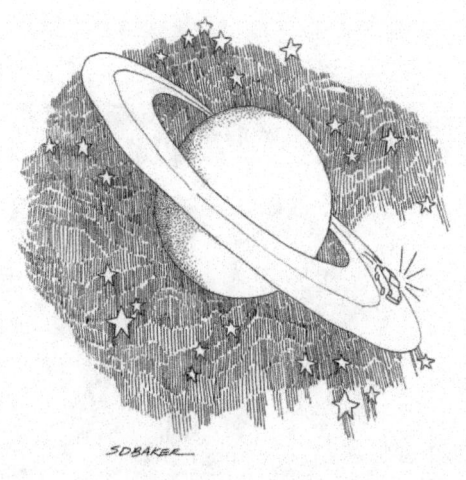

"x#?!#%!!i Darn Kansas Road Map!"

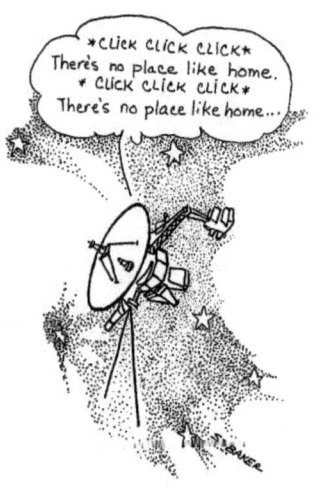

40

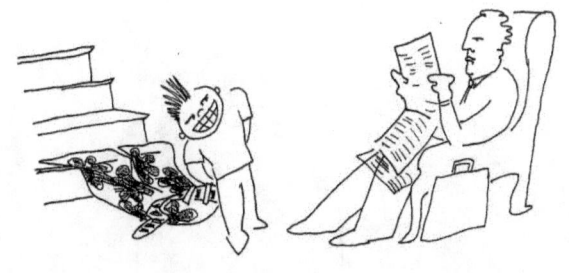

Kids, short on cash? Blackmail your dad with his '68 wardrobe!

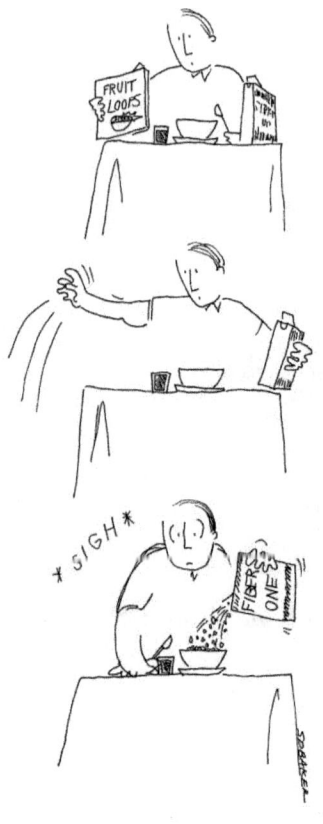

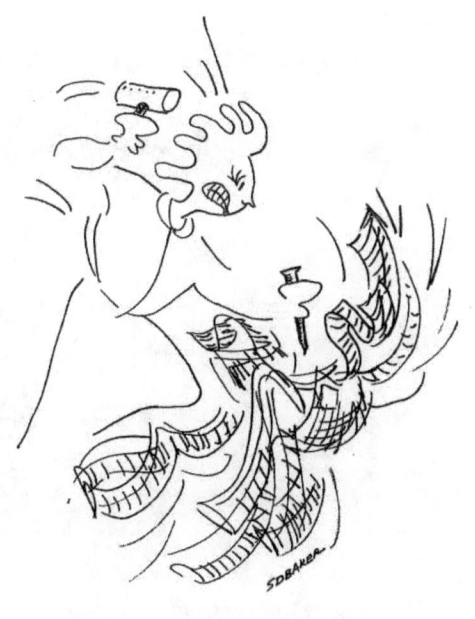

A Housewife's Horror #4:
The Doubleknit that Wouldn't Die

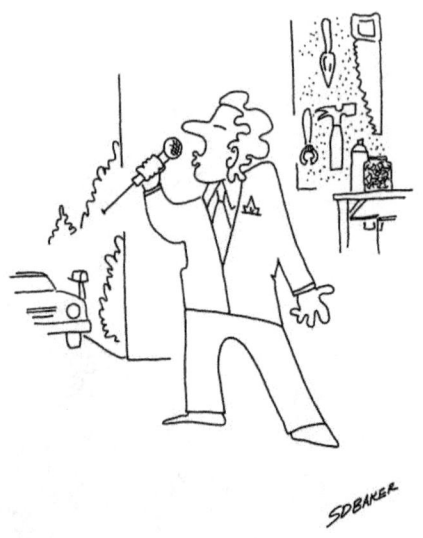

Starting out on weekends in his own garage, Melvin pursues his lifelong dream of becoming a famous lounge lizard.

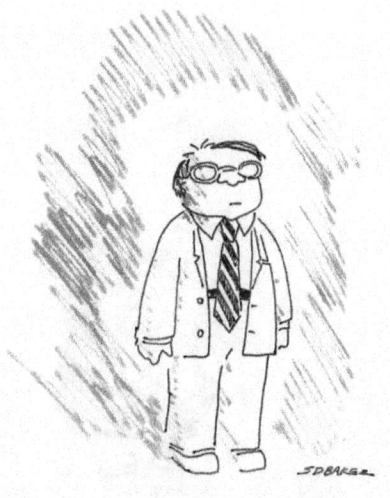

As they asked him one more time how to spell
Prestidigitation, Travis thought back on his childhood.

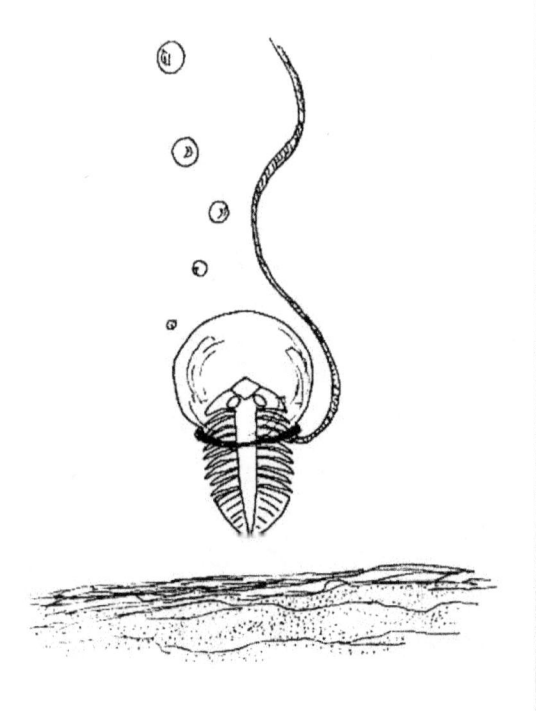

Undersea World of the Trilobite (230,000.000 B.C.,
Before Cousteau)

Happy Holidays!

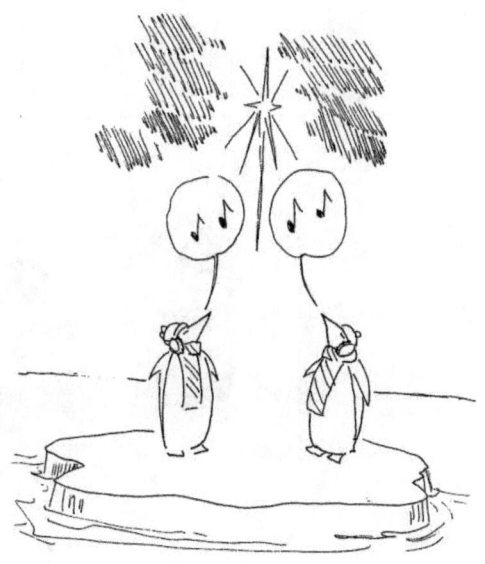

MAP 2
MAGICAL REALISM

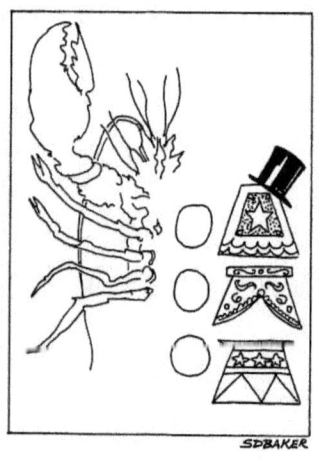

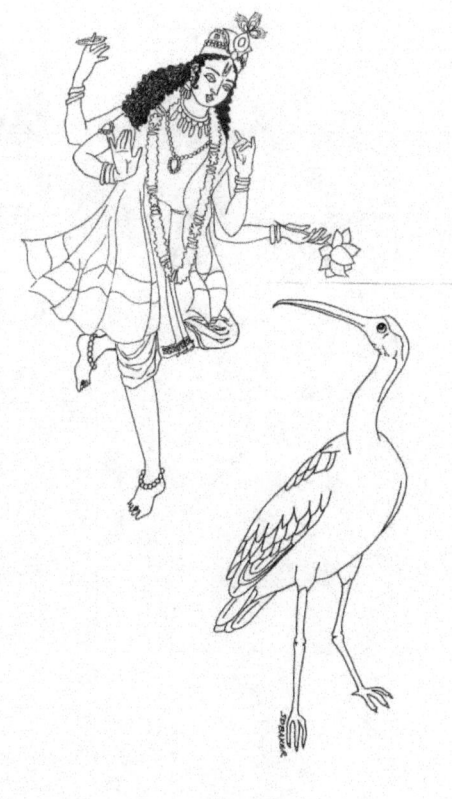

Krishna with Ibis
(First published in MOSAIC, University of California Riverside, 1985)

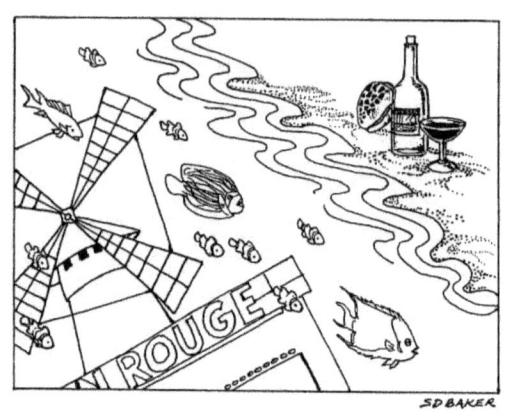

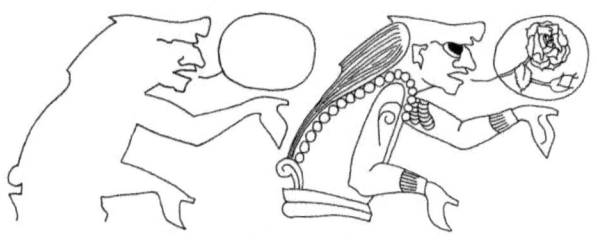

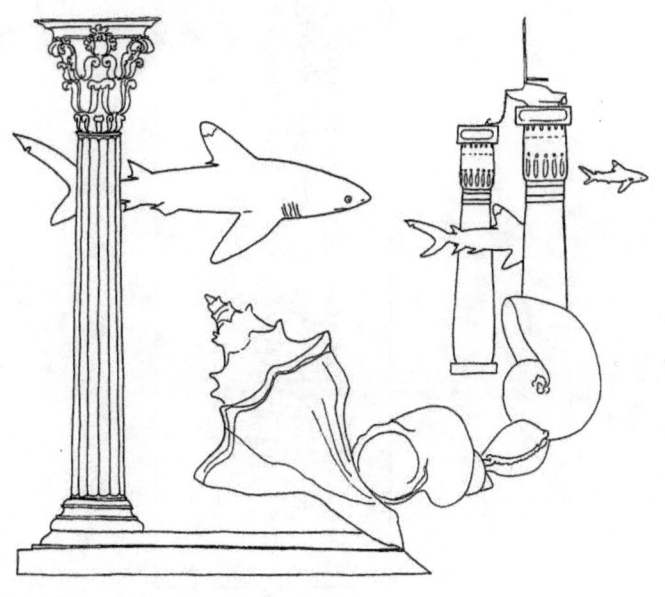

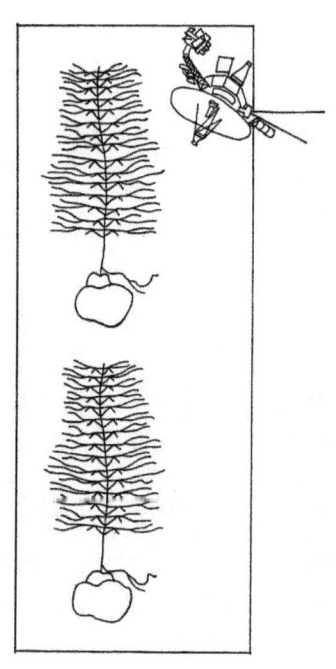

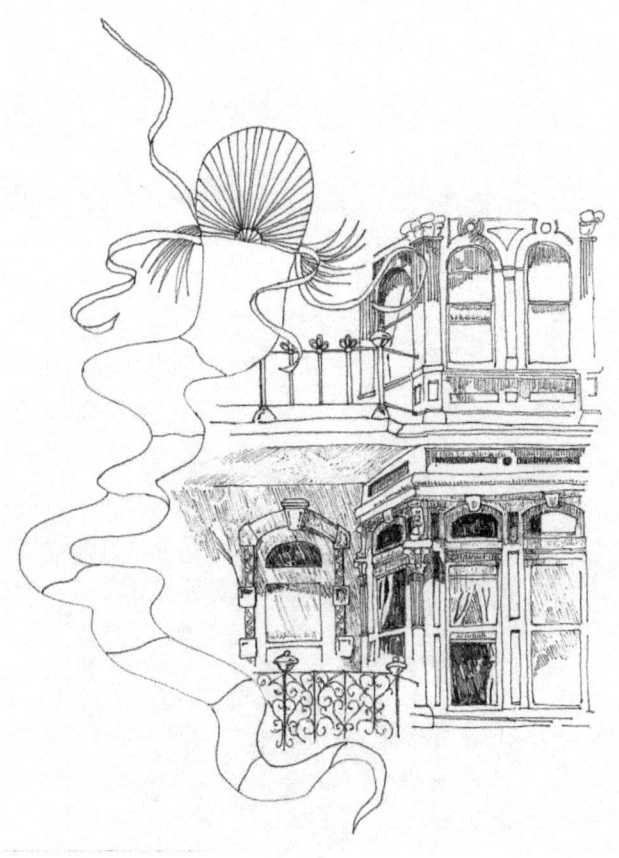

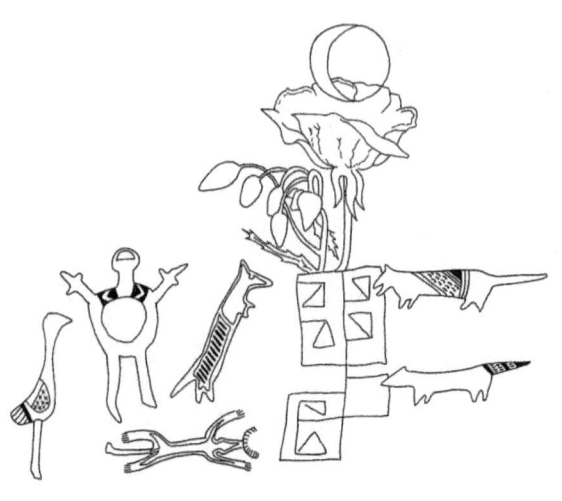

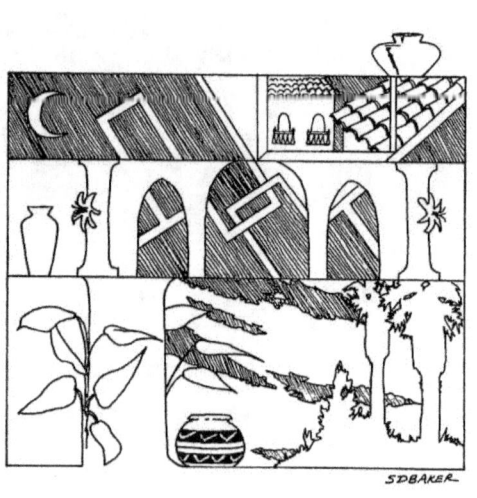

SDBAKER

54

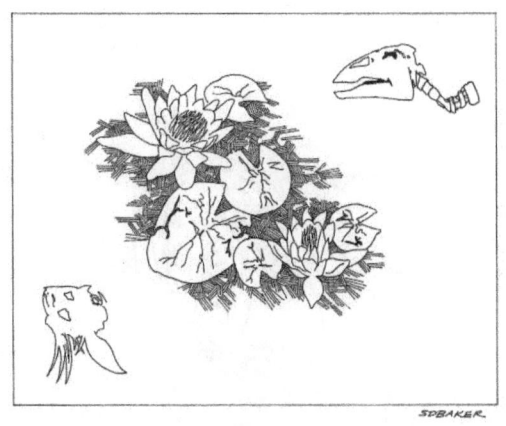

Los Angeles City Park
(First published in *MOSAIC*, University of California Riverside, 1984)

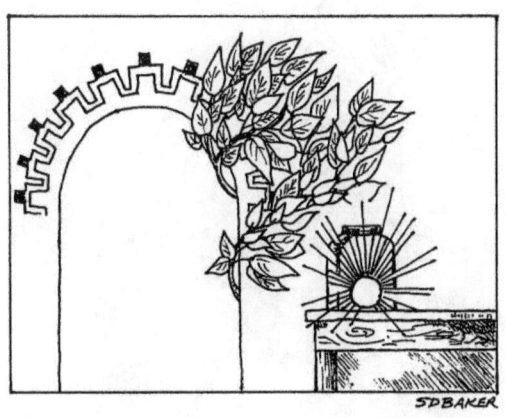

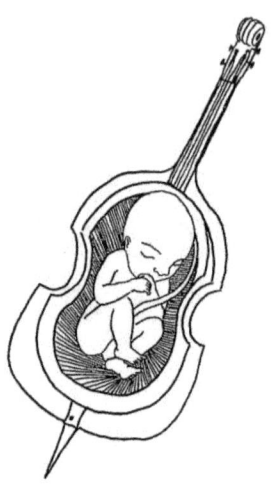

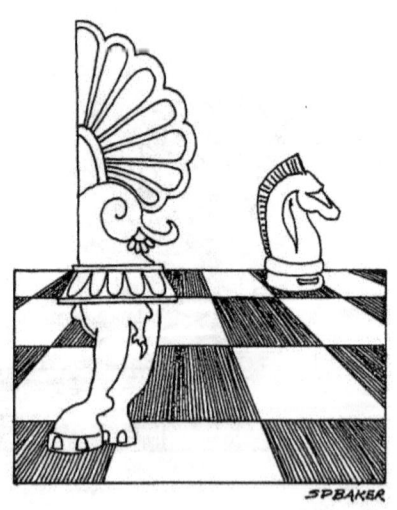

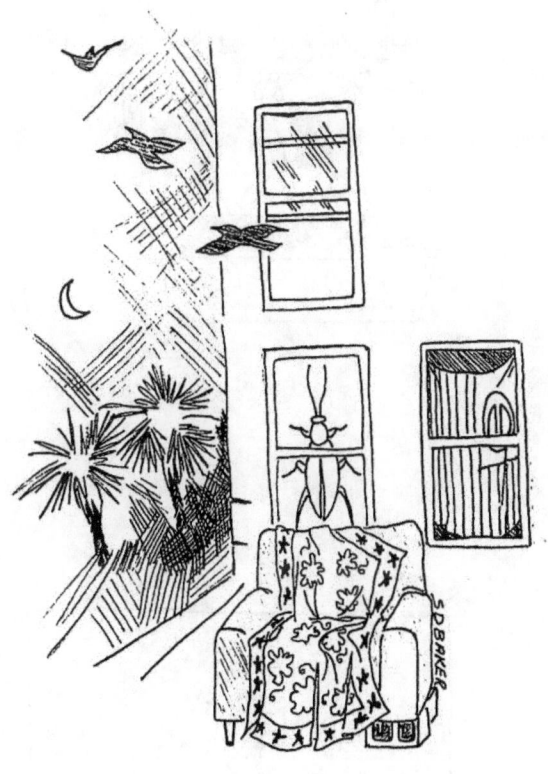

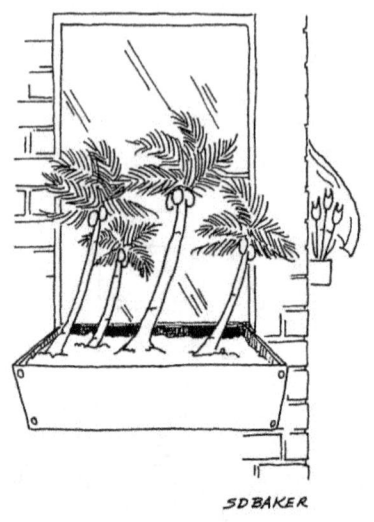

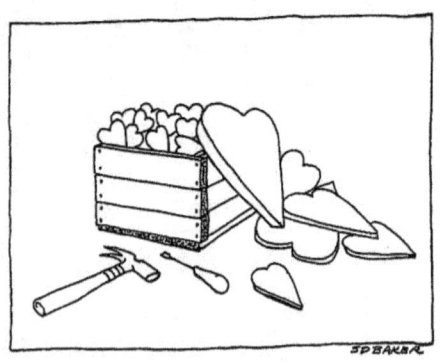

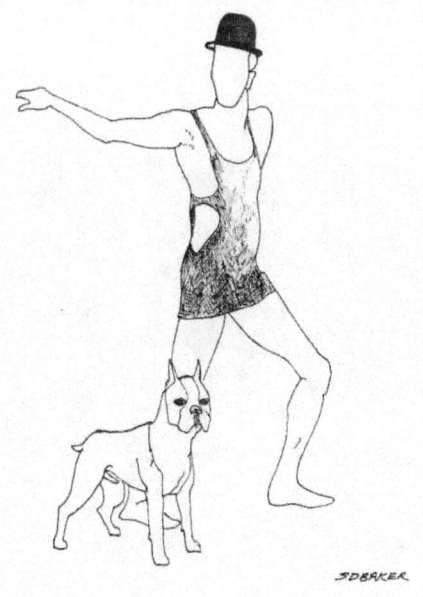

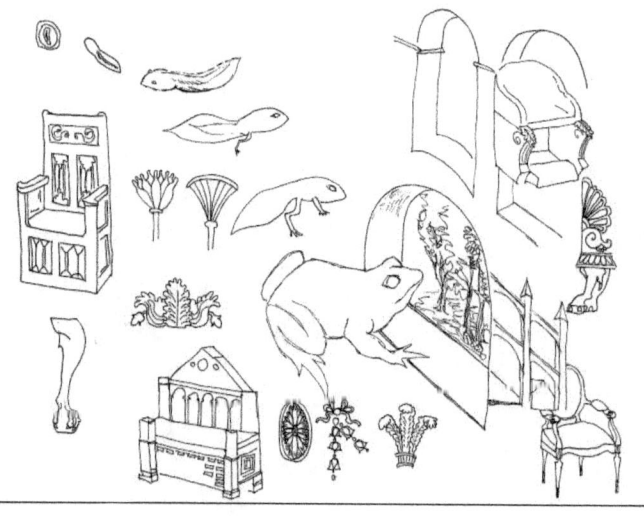

MAP 3
ISLANDS & SEAS

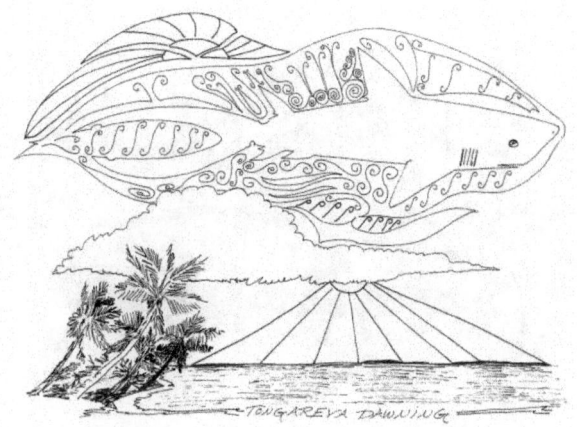

TONGAREVA DAWNING

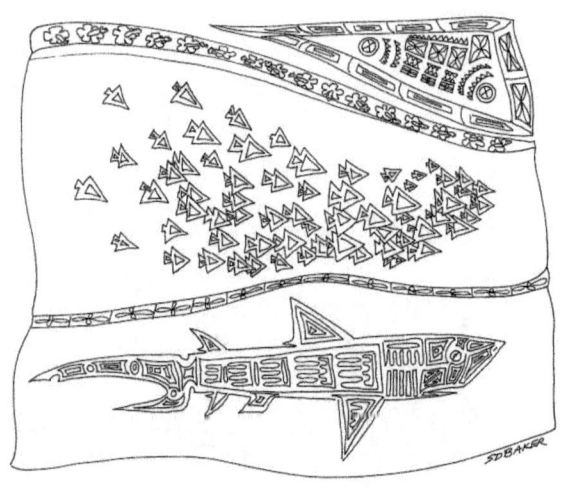

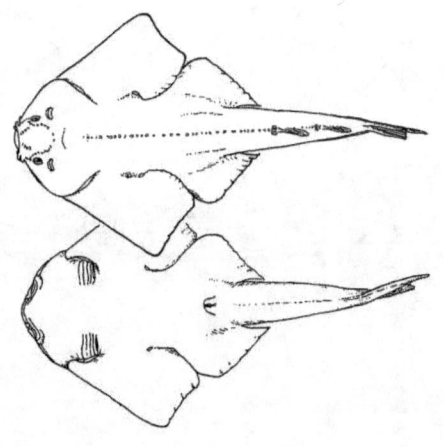

Atlantic Angel Shark (female; After Bigelow & Schroeder, 1948; from <u>Sharks in Question</u>, 1989)

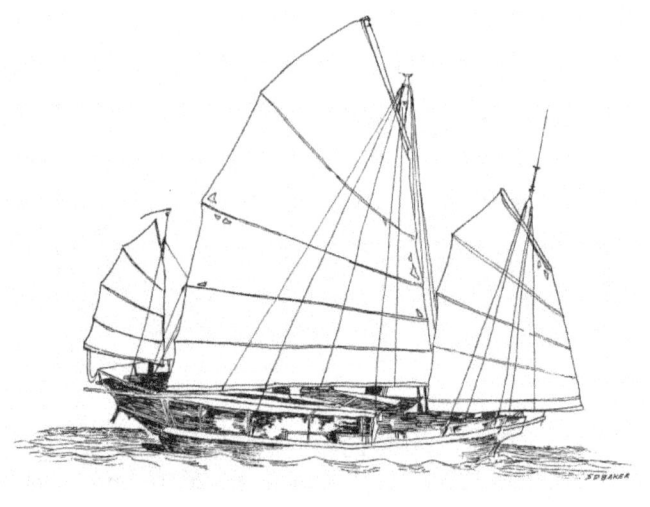

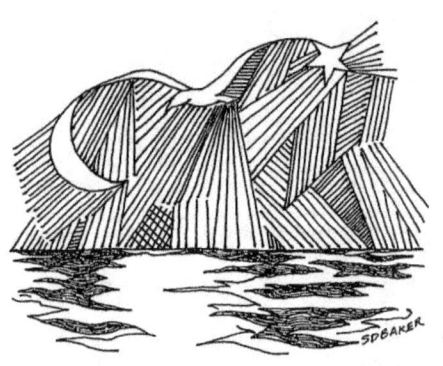

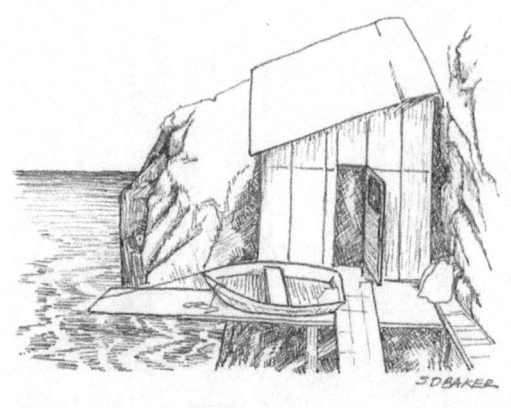

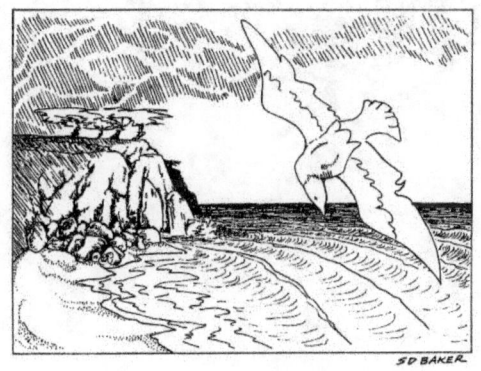

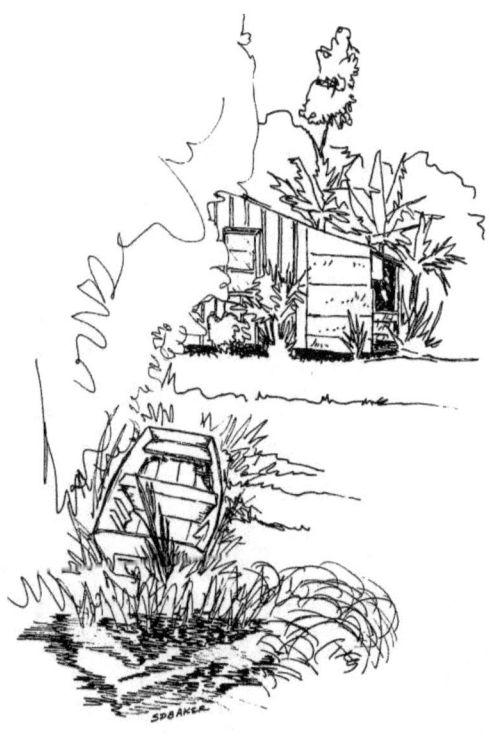

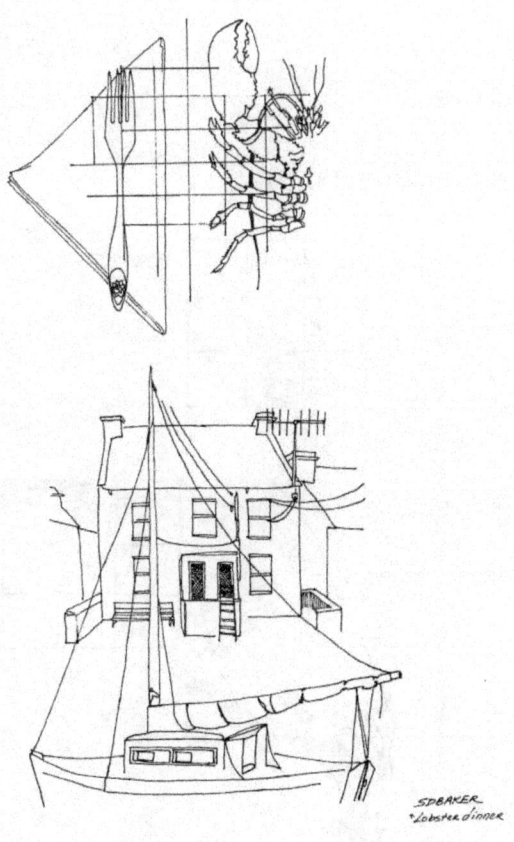

Lobster dinner

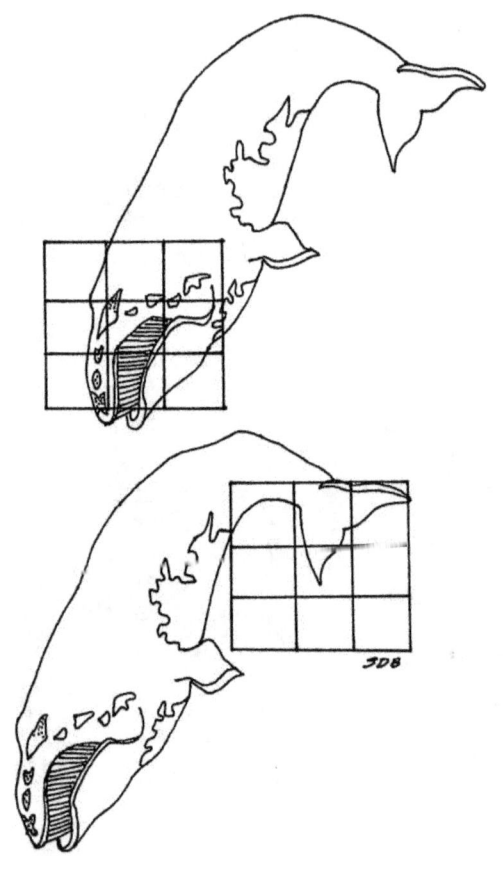

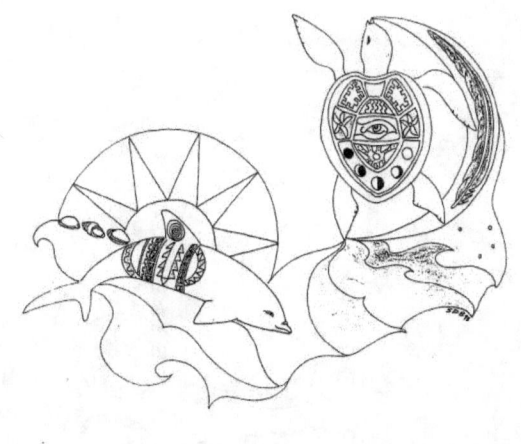

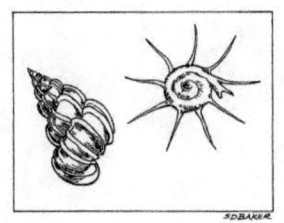

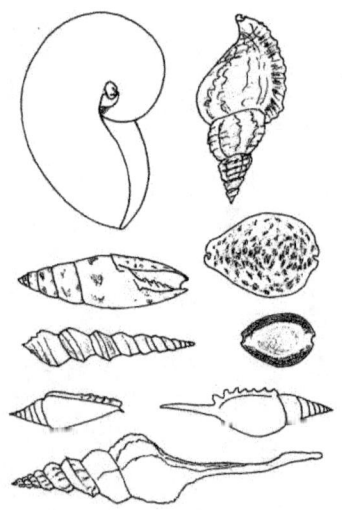

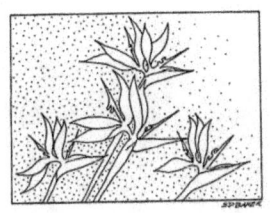

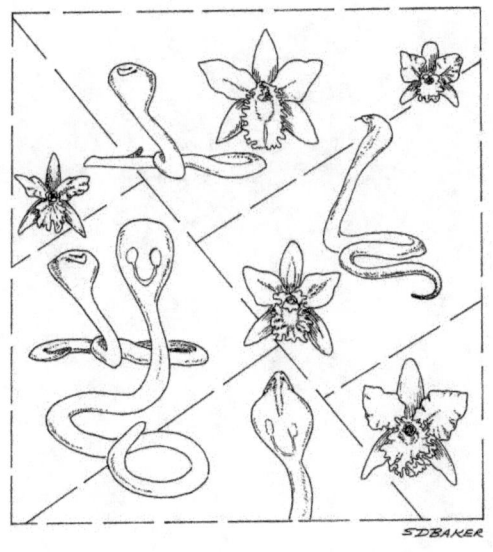

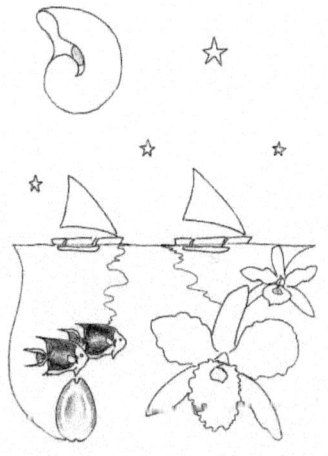

MAP 4
LIFE, OBSERVED

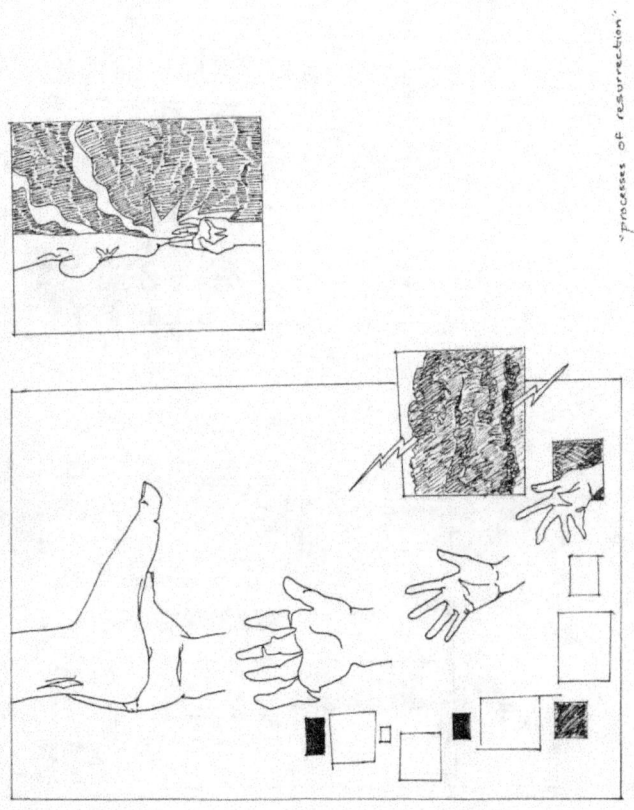

processes of resurrection

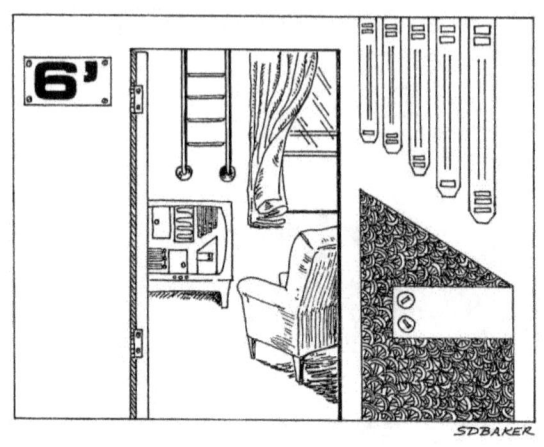

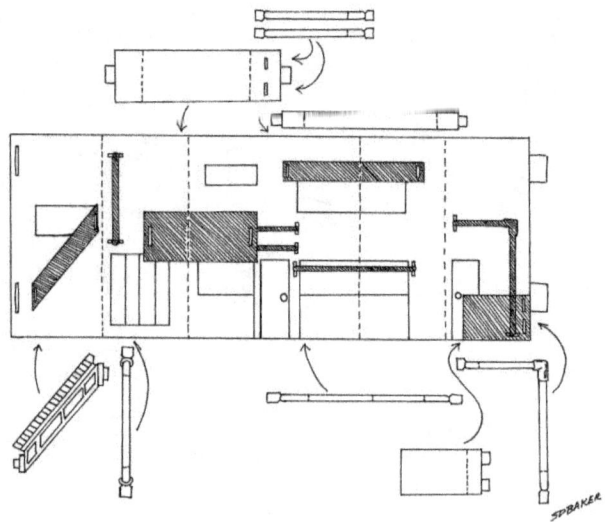

Baby Bauhaus

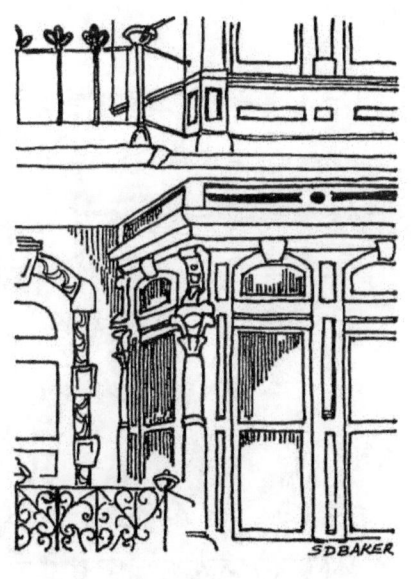

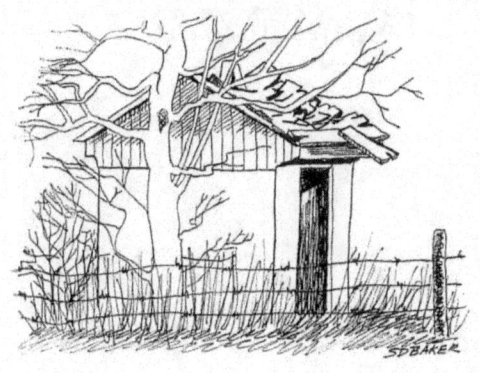

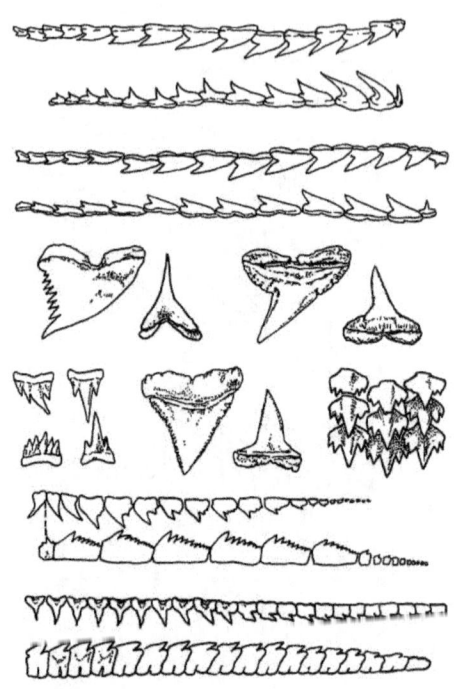

SDBAKER

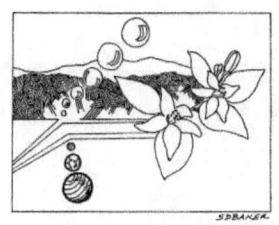

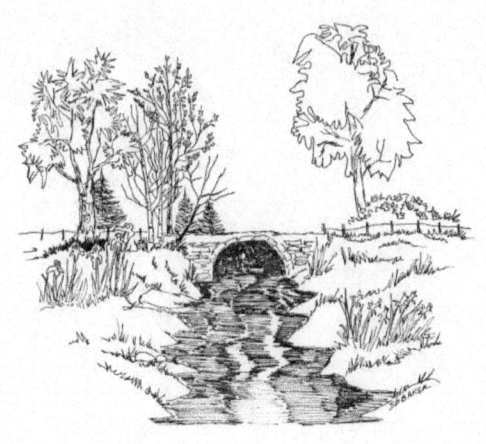

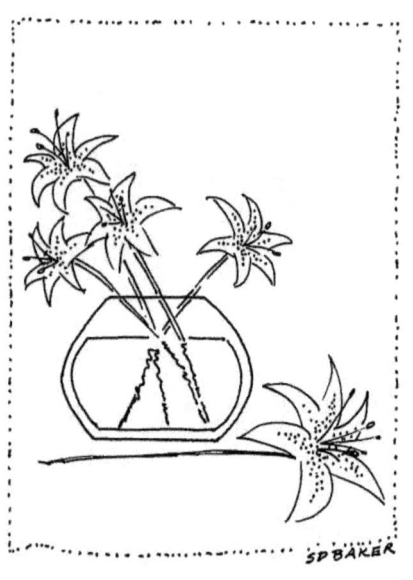

SD BAKER

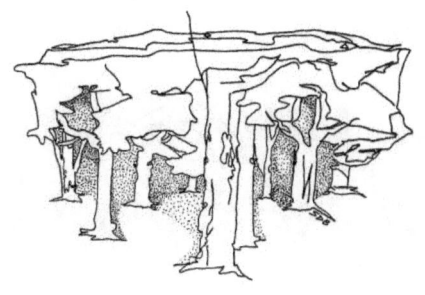

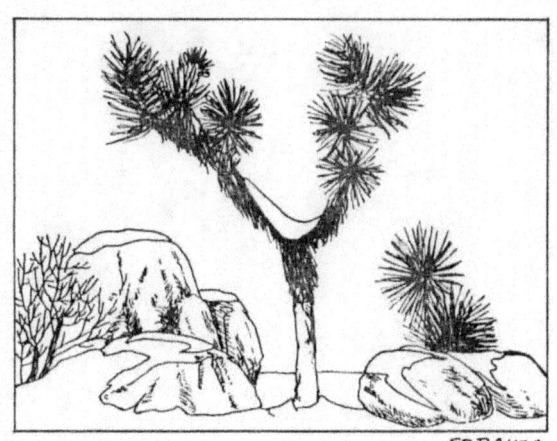

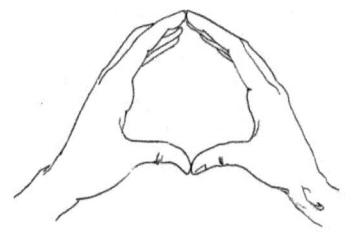

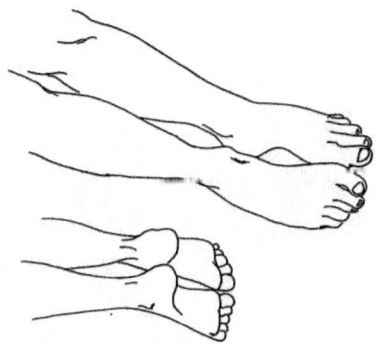

MAP 5
ADVENTURES OF
LITTLE SUSAN

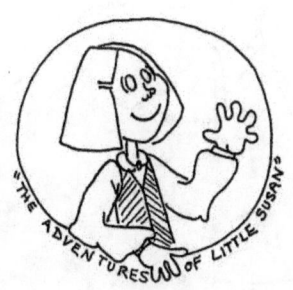

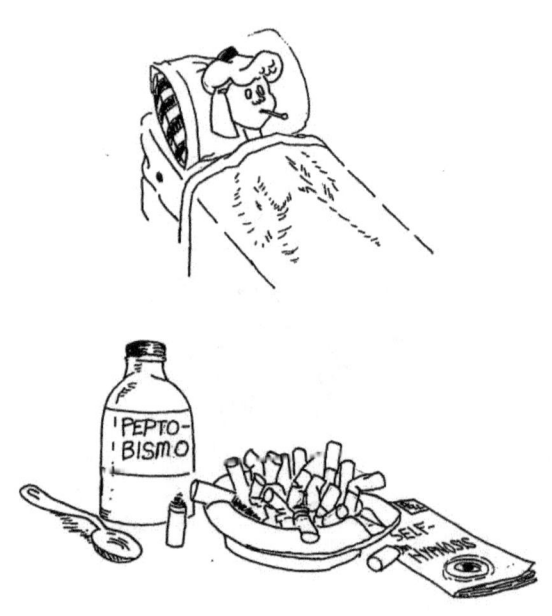

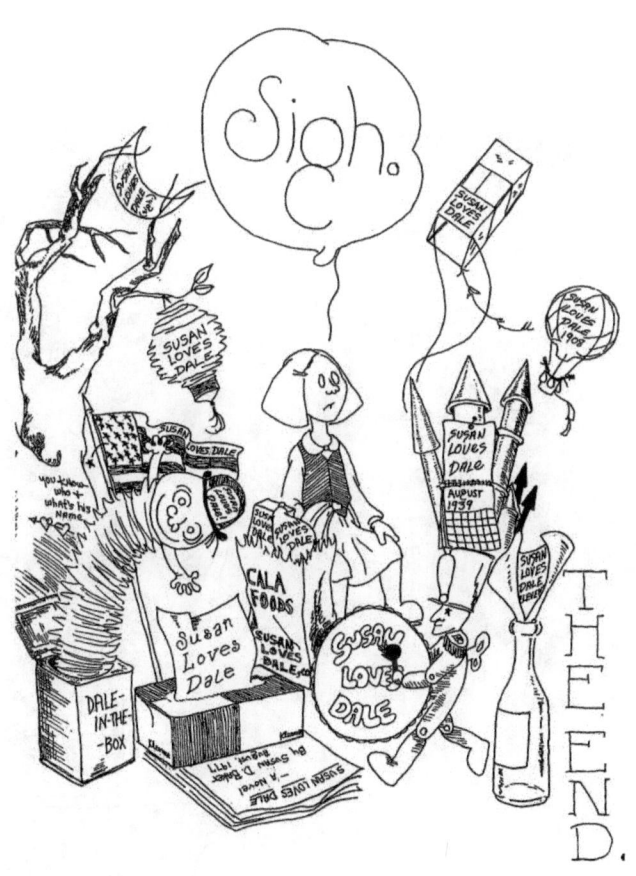

What to do, what to do?

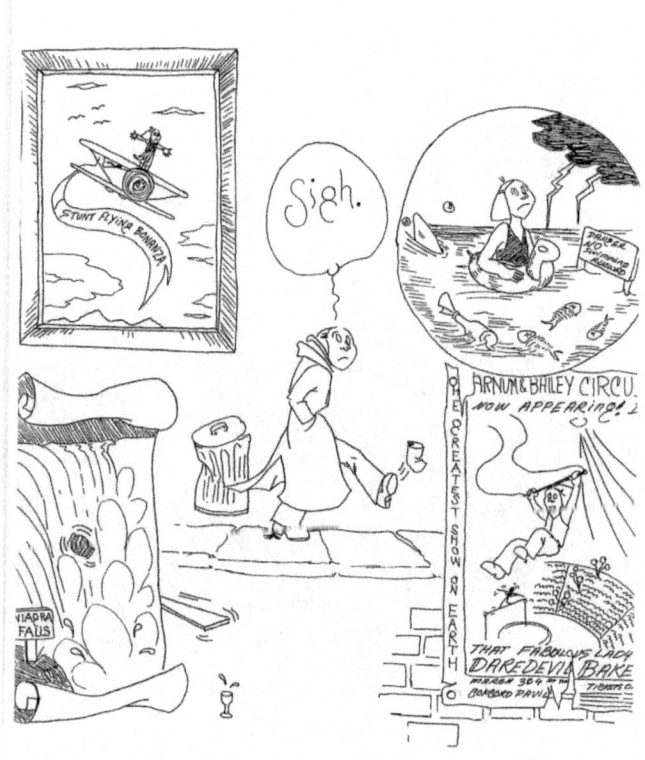

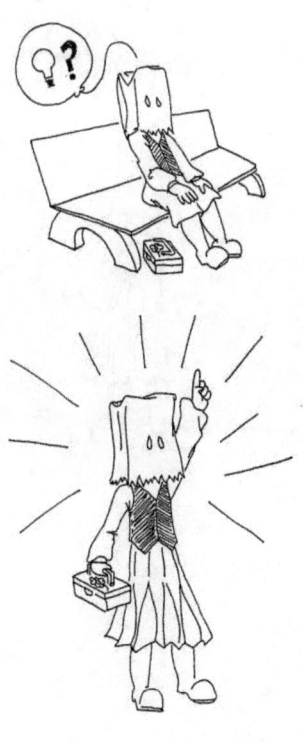

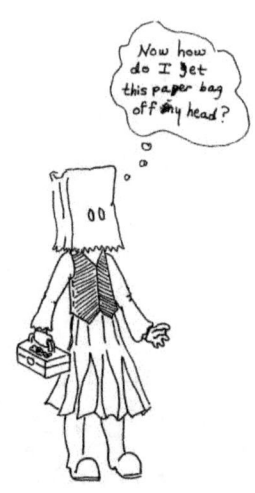

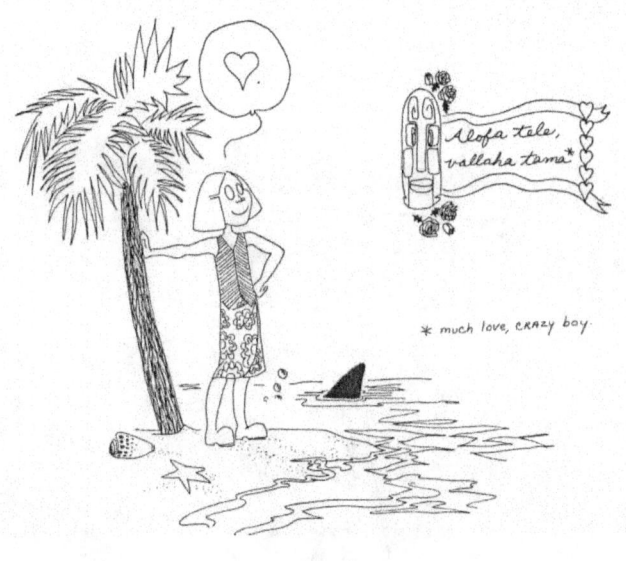

* much love, CRAZY boy

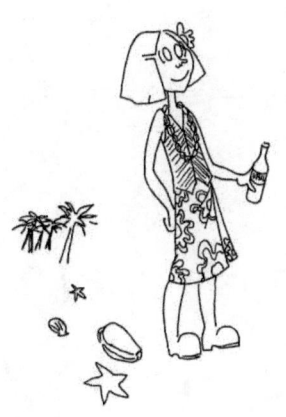

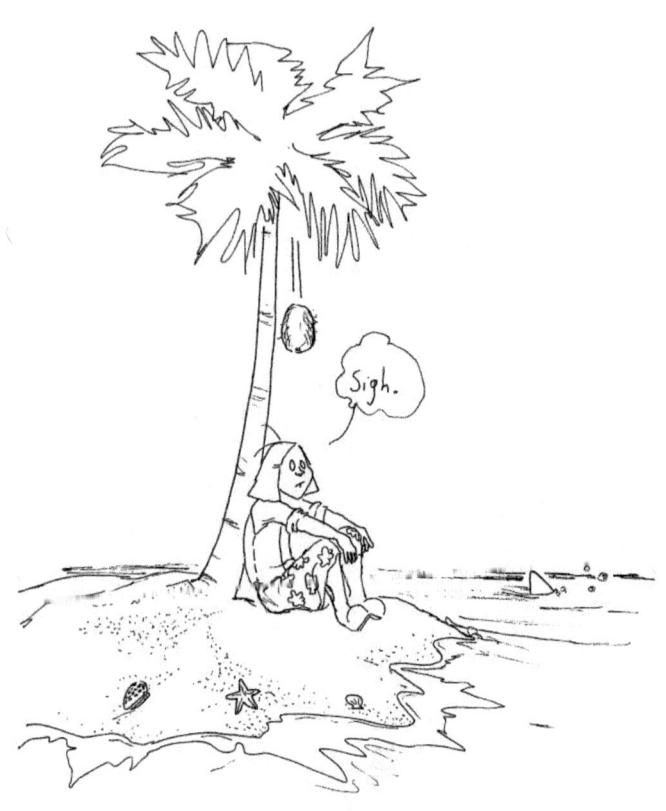

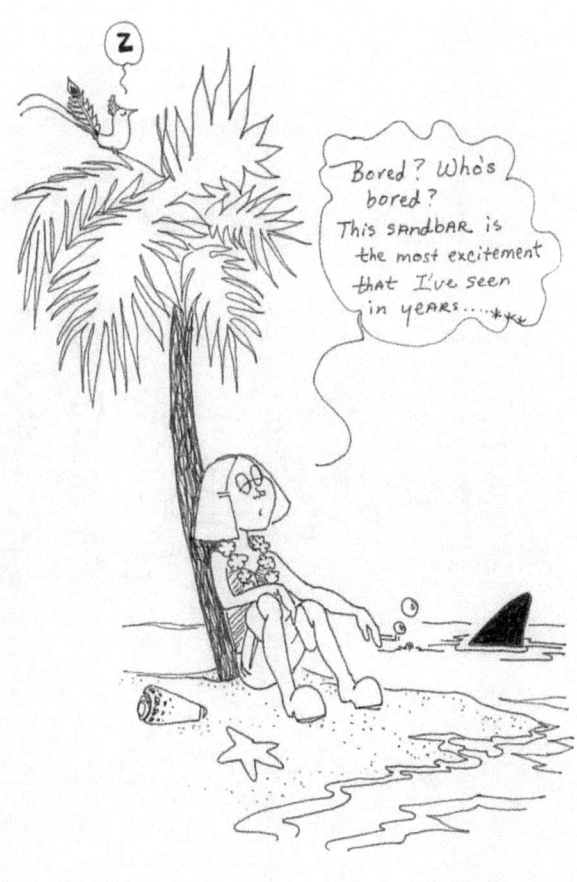

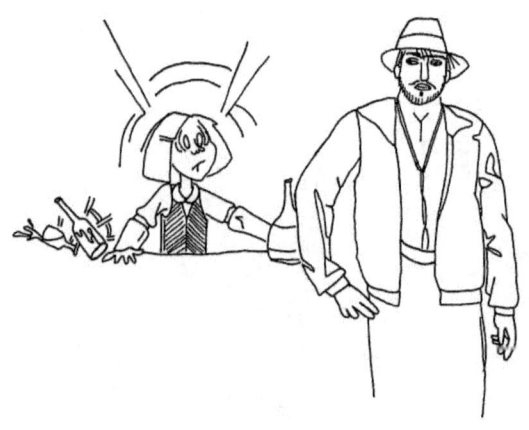

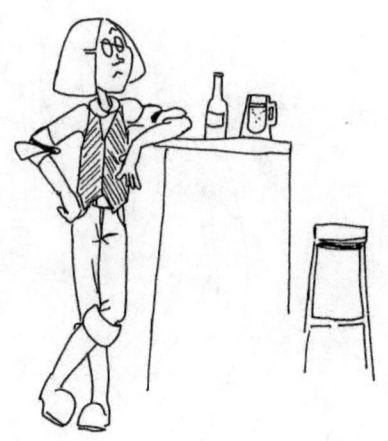

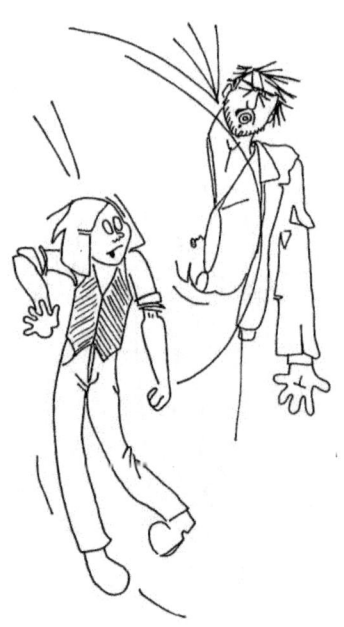

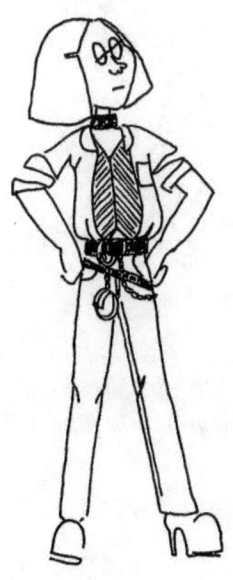

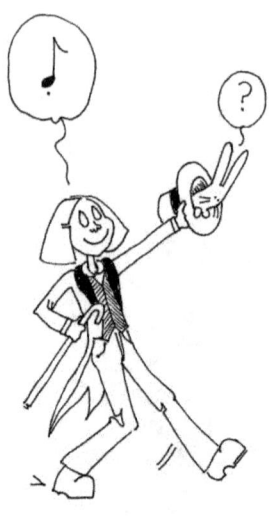

May your days be filled with Happy Foot!

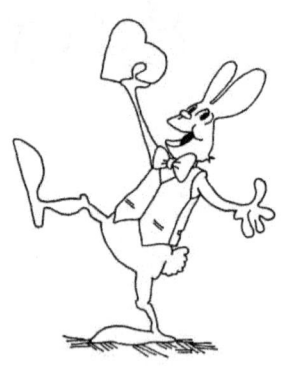

SDBAKER 83

MAP 6
The Sailor

[Short story excerpted from an unpublished novel, *Maps of Water and Hope*]

The smell of wet pork intermingled with decaying island foliage, making it difficult to breathe. Spider Dan stood on the small deck of his boat and opened a Vailima beer. It had become a morning ritual in the Manu'a Islands of Samoa, and he wondered if he had ever consumed so much alcohol on any other island as he had these past few months here, waiting out the steamy typhoon season. He wondered if all his life was measured by motions as dense and secretive as fluids, and, as he gazed out on the hot jungle, he smiled grimly to himself.

Slowly, as if moving underwater, Spider recalled a time in Oahu when he knew he had drunk too much. He always remembered what he did, no matter how much alcohol he consumed, but he often claimed to have no memory, for both of these could serve him. He would cannily know which bars to avoid because of trouble the night before, but if asked, he could feign an innocent forgetfulness, which often helped others forget as well. It was an old trick of alcoholics and he knew it before he had started drinking. Deceit did not bother him. He counted himself lucky to remember, in secret, even when he would rather not. And one memory in particular he would have loved to blot from his mind.

But he could not, for it remained as the final border of his alcoholic limit. He kept it as all sailors kept horizons, as far away as possible, yet always in sight. He had spent an evening with a homesick Samoan friend, and dancing Tongan war dances in a waterfront bar, which he had taught himself to recall with amusement. But he had continued drinking, alone, on his boat offshore, until he had pushed himself to an edge where he felt his body was as liquid as the water beneath the keel. He felt it pull, in and out with the moon, and when a sudden mild rain descended, he thought his flesh turned as rapid and misty as the dark sea. The aquatic transformation both nauseated and elated Spider. He felt he was suffocating and decided to take a night swim.

He knew better; at least, he had once known better. He had felt the seductive rapture of the deep while in the navy, and learned to fear the enticing riptide of suicide in the vast Pacific. But this night seemed to sweep him in a divine reversal of evolution, into the warm tropic sea. He felt his decision was right, and drifted dreamily.

Spider might have been swimming for hours, he had no idea, before he felt the slick pull of a large form in the water below him. It glided just under his legs and vanished, as sensation in dark water often did, leaving the mystery as to whether or not it ever existed. Then he felt it again, far away, more as a presence. A deep sense of belonging engulfed him.

For a moment, Spider thought his blood was exploding, and out of it would come a rainbow of aquatic forms, in every color, like a spray of infinite neon tetras. They would swim across the dark pearl of night, a kaleidoscope of fish in the sky that had become the sea. The moment seemed mystical.

Spider found himself, almost without surprise, half-hoping he would drown. At this time, he felt he could live through it. He felt united with the cleansing ocean that drew in its power to kill from the power it had given to all life. He was now immune to humanity, saved by his surrender of it, and the jealousy that humans held for the ocean, as they stood on frail boats that were not more than shadows. This swim, he decided, was how it should be.

A wild joy entered him, and the underwater form brushed his leg again. The bump was almost friendly. He felt the soothing pull of water displacing the creature as it swam near the surface. Then in the dim boat light, through cloudy eyes, he could make out the unmistakable dorsal fin of a tiger shark.

He would laugh about it later, telling stories of sharks he had briefly "caught" in shallow water, by catching their tails so the thrashing beasts could not turn around. This would become a cheap trick for friends who were also sailors. He would dive beside nurse sharks and marvel at them, discreetly diffident to their lyrical movements, keeping time with the sharks in himself. He would boast about these purifiers of the deep, touch them, respect them. But on that first encounter, he only remembered vomiting whiskey and water on the deck of his boat, then searching out frantically for something else to drink. Anything. Wood alcohol.

He wasn't going to think about it. He was going to drink until he forgot what the touch of his leg had felt like, although it seemed to pain him as deeply as a bite. He decided to drink until the whole world lost clarity, lost sky and night and water, drink until he honestly couldn't remember, and had atoned for his past deceit.

He found a fifth of whiskey and collapsed on his bunk, propping himself up on occasion to drink from the bottle as if it was a medicine, then falling back again. The last thing he recalled was telling himself, this is it, I've done it. Then as he closed his eyes, he imagined tiny demons were running through his veins, infinite demons with sharp pitchforks that they used to spear his blood cells. He could see the cells thrashing, multihued, impaled on these forks, infinite numbers of them in the million miles of his blood vessels, as he lost consciousness.

Now Spider looked at the near-empty beer in his hands. It was late morning, and the sun appeared to dissolve in the hot white sky. The air teemed with mosquitos that seemed to feed off the smoke of rancid pork, rotten leaves and old fruit. Spider labored to breathe.

It did not make sense. The closer he had come to death, the greater he seemed to desire it. He was surprised now to realize that he no longer even feared the rapture of the deep. Perhaps this was the most terrifying of all: somehow, in the past few months, on his battered boat in the backwash of American Samoa, the beauty of it all had won out, without him even knowing it. He opened another Vailima beer and looked back to the faint mist over the island. Within it, for a moment, he thought he saw a dim fragile rainbow rising out of the dank jungle, and disappearing in the clouds.

MAP 7
POEMS

note from a bottle in the midatlantic

no one knows how they get there;
over a thousand miles, the green
sea turtles of brazil swim back   .

to lonely ascension island
lay eggs in the azure mist, and fly
up to the NASA satellite tracking them,

where they leave us cryptic messages
from an alien life form.

i acquired one once
in an antique store
when i bought what i thought
was a map of hidden treasure

i had a choice

among relics of water;

it was either that, or

the pilgrim's flask

from 100 A.D. jerusalem.

someday i will follow

the carefully drawn directions

to my own solitude

sprinkled in blue dust, lost in the sea,

where no one will know

how I got there.

(1984)

Cook's last voyage

i thought it was grace
closing the ocean to each
mirroring lagoon
like the lid of an ornate
music box, but it was only
a memory of silence

from precise longitudes,
on the banner above
the ali'i, the skin
of a parakeet clings
to the inside of gentle
nautilus breezes.

it all turns here, the shell
and the tune, i still recall it,
turning as english clocks
around a gilted sea.

(1984)

pearl divers and prospectors

there are millions of ways
to get lost in the desert, none
to be found, so forget the whisper
of fortunes, the southwest is

half the sea floor, and the sea
where the desert purified itself
to become the sky's mirror,
glittering not with stars but
fool's gold. even if i owned the net

below the water, and hauled
the whole of it aboard, i would surely
drown, and once more pearls

hatch coral snakes
in the trackless, sibilant dunes.

mirrors: cracked and open

this broom you call a body, this
body which is not a body
but a dream you had in bible school
because the heavens were real and body dream
it could do anything

but this broom
is snapped at the handle as smiles are
snapped from the roots of this face
broken as flower stems one does not
carefully cut but pull and bend

this broom has scattered its straw over floors;
dreams that once were parables are
no longer worth recalling: home
in Alaska, blue snows, silence
dark-eyed men

and yet this broom can no longer sweep
them away; I remember

when you are in love

you need not talk

but eyes are lightning in this house of windows

lips are pencils

hands are scented envelopes

legs bend like young trees and speak in the wind

rustle in rain with birdcalls

and this broom

now just wants to jump to the moon

and sweep the gossamer face

gently as a young musician's hand

(1980)

Men

did not invent windows nor ask for herb tea

in the winter; you can see

the tails of brown birds in their eyes

looking in

but women

make glass and cedar chests

they lock themselves up and look out

to the small moon moving in our damp night

in the paisley-shape

of our night

for an answer to the pain

of seeing only

one black hole in men: a pupil

in which they see what is illumed

by their meanings: hot

and dried

we are not opposites, not fenced, and yet

the difference of two slanting eyes

in a face folded over a mirror

seeking out our holes

but the dark mirror of women in a nest

a plush indentation

sucking out the moons of other women

pulling in the eggs dropped

along the arctic sea

in hopes they might yet live

old women in a cedar chest

grow up to hug each other only
when one has lost a child or bought a gift
their shoulders forward as awnings
over crooked breasts

and the roads leading into women
cut against long salamander hills
overlook those cedar homes
on these roads i live
gather
the pieces of straw and rub the small
of my back and wait for night
looking in this straw for a woman's
needle
to write out our ancient alphabets

and put this down as a testament
in the ink of my needlepoint:
all is kind in its sameness
kind in its difference

from one hot rock to another I have swept my hand

now look to the palm

to the flowering start and jagged

finish of a line

Grey Calendars

Sunday, the rainstreets disappeared
in neon spills on a penciled sky;
the value reflections on windows and doors
and jars looked oddly back, beading
in the watery ashes of sun.

Monday, a couple of fruit trees growing
in pots froze over, a shallow moon
in the cold, damp leaves; nothing bloomed
in the beds by the city nostalgia
and old stoplights on Fulton street
but weeds and vegetables.

Tuesday, rolling on buses, escaped
in displays and advertisements;
actors mimed a short parade
in dissident colors
in gutters under
an old dead roof.

Wednesday morning arrived in ochre,
in tame baskets, in dances on Market;
music and toys under yellow umbrellas
fought in the food stamp line –
fighting hydrants and Don't Walk signs.

And Thursday was sullen, forgetful
and lost in schedules of bricks and books;
all our Japanese prints were white on white
on pale, disoriented skies painted
on white and bicycle chains.

Come to me, dark holidays
disfiguring a year, your faces
of crimson and cobalt blue and fragile
double rainbows, snowfalls, growing like
irrational hopes in the street.

(1976)

for bethany: on the issue of our equal rights

is this mind of mine serrated

like a leaf?

does it draw

in sectional exclusion

the green-lipped categories?

but i am a whole

intrinsic unit, a device

for parting the realm of white columns

to pools of light contested by an elm

with sun and shade in constant

hybrid lavender negation

clear as the aged loss of leaves

in wind

i look in the blue

cool downface of a stone

and see my own

i thought I would be a rubber tree leaf

of emerald green, a green impossible to conquer,

regal green, unyielding, that empties

into no stream

but defines the blue pond's granite rim

in the serenity of presence

floating (this way and that, a sudden

             jerk to dark pebble, or light

             as blind november)

i would sing:

      <u>give me the shadow of an elm, the woman</u>

      <u>whom odin carved his hour before the Sleep</u>

      <u>i would take the stately elm, breeding</u>

      <u>green with green in thin-boned beauty</u>

i am but one of millesimal faces

drowned in this body

dense with magnolias

that take off white hands one by

aromatic one

and drop them

quietly

as if seclusion has given us

time, to remove spotted petals

and green leaves

without thought, without a clear

remembrance why

(1981)

a father is not a bodark tree

doctors are monumental liars
circles are thieves

life has brought me back to the
beginning: I have taken 14 steps from left to right
i plant a bodark tree in every footfall

he told me a bodark will live forever
he was ill before i was born

what is this sty in my eye? i've had it
all my life; it's an unassuming curse
to see but not see forests
that spring in the footfall of winter, where the snow
whirls in
imperceptible holes in the garden

in the land of the blind

it was a wooden fence, mouth of wood gaped open

it splintered in the form of rose vines

on the east, left a crack

at the tip of the west as if to speak

roughly on the subject

of bodarks; prickled limbs grew from puddles

of gasoline and fires burned the night

but the bodark grew –

elongated

bolts and chrome

shot from its handcarved crucifix

and when my father could walk he would walk

the garden hose drippling white texas water

on the roots

<u>a bodark will live forever</u>

there's a beam in my eye because i

can't see him; the walker

of bolts and chrome makes out

14 unassuming steps from right to left

i have reached the end of the fence; i want out.

i was promised a land where i counted the trees

under white sun, walked them, fed them hill snow

now a stethoscope hangs on the man's linen chest

a silver crucifix

life is hereditary, i say, it has

no ending. trees do not die, they

dim. i have built a fence and ripped

the outside from the in

i have rubbed

roses on my eyelids to soothe

the pain but the limbs

of bodark trees have cut them

he smiles with daft

appreciation of nothing;

his eyes whirl in

(1981. First published in *MOSAIC*, University of California at Riverside, 1982)

[Editor's note: refers to father's diagnosis with multiple sclerosis]

bird songs and natural abstractions

for Harry Lawton

in the game of invisible
marbles, one child hands me
a fistful of air, i take it,
pass it on to the next, the unseen
exchanged from palm to palm until
somewhere it stops
on the desert horizon. harry it is late

i say, during the malki festival
in the center of the morongo reservation.
the wind stirs up faint galaxies
of dust around the campfire. indian
men are singing of birds; the centuries-old
bird songs drone in the cold night, take
flight, but the stars grind us down
to sand. we crowd in, shivering. harry, i say

on every window ledge of this motel is a cockroach
glaring at me. i fear cockroaches, winged

black feet stomping out dusty galaxies.

they climb in my sleeping bag, slip
out faucets as droplets of gasoline
and flap in the flimsy corners of
this cheap room you have rented us

<u>the desert is where a many-pointed star</u>
<u>fell to earth, rolled over, and dug out rubble</u>

roaches are everywhere, the larvae
of darkness. let me climb off
the floor where they prey, and
into the bed, get out please harry.
i will sleep instead in elevated
calm, dreaming distantly, while you can
live with the unseen roaches in
your favorite motel's carpet.

i will ease you to sleep
with a story about this air:

what it feels like to fly

when you can't land anywhere, or

when you must be invisible:

a story i heard from the desert sky.

you say the bird songs are just like this;

you have studied them, songs by kahuilla

indians at the malki museum.

in the cold dust wind, before

the fire: was i listening, then?

i say i don't understand

kahuilla, but i have an instinct

for preservation

(1984)

[Editor's note: Harry Lawton – journalist, author of *Willie Boy: a Desert Manhunt*, and advocate of the Malki Museum - was Susan's mentor and friend]

exegesis of eden: an encounter with <u>Marina</u> and <u>Samoan Lullaby</u>

With special thanks to T. S. Eliot and Suzan Bokanovich

Tutuila Island, 1981

what seas what shores what islands burning blue

become white; the long quill

dropped down to make a world upon the world

returns to me and yet returns to

bird who is no more

above the water

…

i walked on burning feather on the sea

on coral walls

on shells involute, sea-pink;

i saw escarpments of wind untouched by light

and white clouds cleft with sun

burning the rachis of banana palm

we return to our gods

in every song:

Pele cracks out her love and fear of sea

and when the feather falls from beating wing

she told me how a spirit will

rise up from deep benthonic voice

and find its way to the harbor; we are pained

by that which has no place to return but hers

in archipelago

<u>where all the waters meet</u>

…

degrees of this island are measured by

the oar of Rainmaker mountain in the wind

where earth and sea cry out for compliment

in that dim blue meaning

Death

down in gilted rain or up the sun's hard path

we move this power of life on burning mountain

to make a monument

in that dim blue meaning

Death

has the boat detached itself from the marina

to walk into heaven refracted on a whale

as one moves through the island bush

burden by the axes of trees?

what seas and shores have spawned this memory:

Matafao and her hands of taro leaf

clapping in fever to lay her hands on hands

and offers the verdant breast to

small birds etched in bronze sky

do not look back

my fruit, my daughter, my friend

grace is not desolate, beatitude lean

and the smoke of the umu on Sunday

is too heavy for the wind

...

birds become unsubstantial

faded in the cornea of clouds

i am given seeds that have no names and eyes

that hang the night below a tepid rain

in her dark hand she holds the nitid

southern cross

to burn away winter

burn away the fog

and trap in these embers fire: incurable

scintillant and rising over waves

she found the plume and learned to fly away

my daughter whom i have become

reeling in silk from my hand

you were born to make the fine mat, drink

the kava

reel in sounds of others

and write out warm, benthonic song

for Matafao

and the battered sands

...

they will give you reason

    the falatasi is empty, one long smile of wood

they give you reason

    boats are netted in harbor, sunk in, under april
moon

they give you hope:

not island, sand nor sea

but only this memory

dropped out slow, for a god who does not

care to count his plumaged thoughts

has dropped us

carelessly: windcarvers, sailors, users of wood and
shell

dropped down in florid profusion, blessed here, alone

and convoluted, unaware

that oceans have trembled here

when touched by that white plume

we will stamp out a wing

<u>i must leave this water</u>

stamp out a wing

<u>and let this water</u>
<u>be</u>
<u>in its soft husk of coral and sand</u>

we stamp out wings on our backs and cross

the great water

...

we were born from feather of birds who wreathed the
sky

and return to birds

leaving our boats to scratch the marina

leaving our coconut smoke and mountain

in pluvial shadows and sienna wood

rise up the life for life, speech for the unspoken

i was split by the knife but did not know this

until i slept the hour of knives in your green hull

cut open the hour and time, reciprocal

will open a porthole

i must find holes in the water

must find holes in my winter

i have cursed in my dry throat the elements

i have been expunged by the elements

i have slept below louvered windows all my life

and looked out on tin roof imitating sun

but did not know it

until i slept in your fanned falis and saw the strobe

of tropic sun

on corrugated tin and then

i knew it

i have bent below dripping palm trees all my life

and felt my pulse in shaded afternoon

and heard the meaning of Death

but did not know it

until i crawled in your dank wilderness

and heard my beating heart in your dim blue

and knew the meaning of it

under the cracked beam of evening

when i had nothing to lose nor left to throw away

i wondered if there had been april moons

on marina

all my life: to sink in

all my life

and walk out the white hole to heaven

ride the great Wing of light

...

what seas what shores what islands now burn blue

in the distance of yesterday and tomorrow

as i walk between the daylight and the daylight

in the guileless eden of Samoa

a bird has made a raft and makes no more.

(1981)

Dynamite Fishing
Pago Pago, American Samoa

Video games again. Hibiscus blooms
on each boy's slender hips. Below the fan
I hear a gecko tap its ironclad shoe
on the hulls of sunken ships
resounding through the tapa-shrouded rooms.
The boys lean under the black glass. Turbine sand
blasts clean the harbor, paints it ocean blue.

The noise is deafening. In each boy's hand
a firecracker floats to fish-pail seas
where once kalia raised enormous sails
against the wind; now tuna factories
spill out a glittering refuse: fins and scales,
Saint Peter's coin fish, drifting down the dark
into the sanctum-silent mouth of shark.

(1986)

for all of oceania

there are spiders hatching in my lungs;
it is difficult to breathe
in humid weather, and webs cling
to the green rift off a coastline.

it is hard to get drunk
at sea level near the equator but
enough alcohol will fill
the blood outward;
there is always
enough; the palm trees carry
brown spider sacks
and the rain burns up
from the jungle.

we can get drunk in los angeles
and breathe in the perfume of micronesians from the
white desk
of an airline. but they do not appear to be
moving, suspended like island relocations,

in the night clouds cold and high

i heard there were nets

in los angeles harbor meant to keep out

sharks

but have trapped instead

the tuna and dolphins,

corpses in motionless swim

attracting sharks

to the tangled white fence;

we stroke their bitten bodies

with our metal gloves

one hand on the ocean holding it

back

one hand on the stillness

of the heart

(1984)

elegies for nuclear test sites

1/eniwetok atoll

eniwetok breathes in pastel

apertures

that rise from the silt underlining to lucid

lagoon

in fingers pricked for blood

examinations

turns in aerated wave in fine

disturbance of undertow

and we pull out, out: away from arboreal island

out the south channel, passed Igurin

toward the glittering path of naval of the moon

but crystal tubes below

blue sheen of water

continue to bleed

in us and through us, the unseen

serums, acute and complex

as channels of the heart.

breath is the simple

holding of a hand to chest wall,

or water in the lull

of coral reef

the silk route

somewhere in kashmir she wears this
silver necklace still. it is the same east
that touches the west with a chain
of lilac incense, it is the same silver

from neck to neck. in the year of the snake,
her face was reflected in dal lake
with the setting moon. they were twins

who saw each other, believed the other
held one end of the pole secure,
and she the original could spin
the earth below her feet

in the conceit of silver. under
the lapis night, she spun into both
basket and the hooded cobra within;
she felt each strike, and the chanting

silk silk, on the fragile highway,

on the drum sky over the himalayas
beaten by sticks of icy starlight.

nature hides rivals of ourselves
in snow, what becomes of it, even
in this lotus garden. we drift our
chains in the lakebed, thoughts dark
and forsaken. old ghosts bled
between concepts of heaven and hell
beat the silver drum in water
hoping to pierce the surface and begin
where the flow begins.

there is only this tragedy of ghosts
she left from the east, her smile benign.
the silver twists. it alone remembers.

(1984)

tanka: the santa ana winds

lost condors circle

a desert filling station;

bored children call them

spirits of coyotes and

fire handguns at their eyes.

plum leaves in wind

plum leaves in wind

bruise-blue, are startled by the messages

of birds; a delicate branch

wavers

as if branches were made to quiver, thin

pale unformed bones; an ivory

twig will bend and snap

and shed its plum leaves

scattering

purple scrolls on which bird messages were written

or perhaps thin tongues which have heard the Word

of sky; secret, inviolable

jealous of its everlasting

blue difference, sky separates itself

up the shaft of any point or tree

but wind cradles plum leaves

participants in grace

and receivers of bird-visions; dark plum pages

are etched in innocence: by holy order

that which bends and snaps by holy

orders itself like words in a language:

at first illegible but then extreme

in desire to make one thing as perfect as the next

serene and inescapable

so pass on these analogous notes;

a dance will throw itself heavenward

leaving perhaps the dancers to fall away

the plum leaf papyrus for one second

drops

allowing itself to shake out

fragile steps learned from the cirrostratus birds

or to test that plum-violet, a memory

a purple hue

so much like the sky's blood or where

the sky has secretly bled

in the rite of late evening

when the sun is crucified.

(1982. First published in *MOSAIC*, University of California at Riverside, 1982)

first theory: splitting the atom

for Lise Meitner, physicist, who mathematically discovered
nuclear fission, 1918

in the days when uranium was

the new tundra

and an atom

the last sterile seed

in the territory of the unknown

night to night sewn

you parted them

to see the principle:

the sun beyond the velvet curtain

clear to the mind of a mathematician

as aurora borealis

in the night sky

there must be a color to dense

polar snow

scent to the unpredictable

blue rose

and a beam of light

through the tiniest crack

in an early spring window

somehow a circle has been made complete

and drawn back like a mouth

in fission

(1982. First published in *MOSAIC*, University of California at
Riverside, 1982)

Your aversion for the color red

for Wayne

"Is the enlightened man subject to the laws of causation?"

Zen koan

a line of ants stops to argue

which one is closer to the moon

as they advance across the face

on a coin reflecting the moonlight

fields are dense with foxtails

I carry in my hands, the nails

with which you empathize, and yet

we have all sinned against

this peculiar winter night

when the lambs, frostbit as marble,

graze the peripheral sight,

or sleep in white hospital beds

rising and falling like thirty silver

coins of moon. Where are you?

Awake at 3 a.m., crouched on the icy

kitchen floor, drawing flowers on each stone

over my bone, flowers for the joint and muscle

given away at dawn. The bougainvillea

drop red petals over each

grave in the hospital garden

where the zen master meditates

a discourse on emptiness;

we who are about to die

are thankful. The incarnations

of foxes hang in my closet

like dark lace gowns. In fields

coyotes circle statues of sheep;

under the foxtails, red ants prowl.

This is sin, not an illusion

and every coin is someday

spent on a potter's field. So let

your aversion to the color red

melt down into a badge of courage

to be human, too,

and pin the self straight through

on the sleeve of sun.

(1984. First published in *Caliban*, 1991)

Zydeco

On the old accordion you will hear
African rhythm, Celtic vocals,
but invaders' Latin, taken as a child
once stolen from the back of an army tent.
Initiated into our tribe, adorned
with lion's teeth, he was given
the wind colors, vibrant or
misty, that make living spirals in the sky
inspired by the music of the spheres.
And years later, when he returns
to the Order of the Leaden Crucifix,
he carries with him
a snake egg, and a gris-gris bag,
and talks to the trees in his sleep.

(1990)

Ode to Human Origins (Growing Upper)

for Jules Ardis, formerly of Riverside Community College

We began as walruses

looking backward. Well maybe that's not

the truth of evolution, but neither is

Jacob's ladder, which he saw

when he was wrestling with sharks, not

angels. Angels live in thimbles of the Nile

tossed over, perfumed alabaster boxes,

not on the rope of higher evolutions

which is what we are supposed to be doing

with ladders. Sharks, however,

that lurk in the mud of every story

of evolution, looking forward,

are worthy opponents! Not ethereal perfection

in route from hell to heaven, back again,

hip heavy, with masterly reports

written with diamonds on a glass wing.

Sharks

bleed, have we forgotten, and sense us

as first mothers, moving above the mud line, ever
moving on those serious two feet, our thumbs
preoccupied, our brains about midway up
the chimney to saturn. Hey, it's a start.
We evolved from sharks

or should have. Ladders
are circular in nature, not ascending
nor descending, they are laced around

the fingers of confounding children
on a back porch. With a flashlight you left out

because it's going to storm, dammit, or an
earthquake is predicted, and now the batteries
weaken to speak with fireflies, in the density
of giggles, as sound might move

underwater – yes you have it:
the lifeline back to our own creation.

or at least to the moment you stood in a store

hoping for matches, maybe, but actually (looking) at

switchplates, with funny non-noises, or alabaster
boxes of

  circuitry

that would make whirs and fizzes if you hooked them
up

  just so, if you only remembered, but you saw it last

in a dream, and now the floor is shaking

your child is scream-laughing, the porch light

explores, fireflies

flood your dark aqua window

and you are out in the middle of the ocean, in a boat

with tangled thumbs of rigging, and the quiet dorsals

of sharks as nuns surrounding

and what have you done?

Where has that child (in you and from you) gone?

And why is evolution

so tangled, contemplative, messy,

mired in philosophy, so like a shark, really, impatient

to be wrestled, to move cloudy water through the
gills,
draw in elements of life, expel
the nonorganic? And why do you see
in each shark's eye
not your own anymore – you expected that – but
itty bitty rope puzzles! Kids' crinkled feet
as they fly on the waves of bioluminescence,
and those sharks entwining – grab a shark!
Struggle with him! See the jagged gleam!
The loops and cradles! And such a dream

as we all had that last night
with a squaredancing shark
a child in a lab coat
bottles and tubes and block and tackled and curious
liquids and whistles and beeps that suddenly all went
POOF.

(1992)

I AM THE BODARK

They say the bodark has no eyes.

No skin, just featureless

form and disposition of fire

and wood and firewood

and those horseapples, soft as bruises

to the wind.

I am the bodark.

The old tree, the crippled tree

under the olive Texas sun, the only

one still living tree

where the fires burned half the night.

Someday, a tree of ash

And living light

For no shadow will remain

To cast on these white slate rocks

no shadow and no emptiness,

only light to scatter, light to rest

as white petals falling down the sunlit sky

into my shape, the bodark

crippled and bent, old and grey,

what is left of tomorrow

burning within me

    cut open the hour, and time, reciprocal, will give us a portal

the gasoline

fires of the night

all doctors are still liars,

but not all circles are thieves.

They will circle and stop and point

and say to the next generation: *this is the tree,*

the tree without peace, the tree with no skin,

the tree with troubles, the tree I flame.

(same stanza)

Then they'll take a snapshot. TREE.

(Trees that speak will burst into fire, for)

to speak is to know what happened to my name

to speak is to know my name
and why I am here.

But it isn't me, it isn't me,
I'm gone with the dawn,
with the Light; the dying tree resurrected
the one last tree felled from the pinnacle of Texas
toppled, fallen, cast down, fruitless
old bodark with briny sap, thorns, weedy,
old bodark walking with an Easter hat on,
old bodark walking into light.

———

nerves speak
making a new circumference
to Saturn, trapped
within the barbed-wire jaws
barbed-wire lives; a crumpled ball of barbed wire
hurled into the next millennium, where someone
catches it,

hurls it back.

That's Saturn.

Too bad Marx was not a poet. They will say,

Too bad he was not a poet.

Too bad.

(new stanza)

And what do your nerves say? They ask me,

What do they say, little lady?

They tell me the color of your eyes within,

the color of your eyes within.

This could end, very soon, they answer, or they warn,

there is no difference; *over very soon,*

if you give us the secret combination to your lock,

the one you've kept all these years.

The one you've never given away.

End very soon. Very soon. Soon.

Why is there a sty in my eye? Help me, I say,

to pluck out this seed of Babel, this strange non-light.

A different color in the circle of his eyes,

A different color behind his stethoscope,

rotating inward, monochromatic, a color of dreams,

it's time's rotation, faster than Saturn, faster

than circles, faster

than doctors. If I could stop the rotation, if

I could see within the color, if

I could see at all, perhaps I could

answer them. But the sun is on its

own journey, the light stops for

no one's name. The white Texas water doesn't

come as often, anymore, now, here.

And stops for no one's name.

———

In a dream, I am surrounded

by gardenias drifting

out of the sky. In a dream

I am a small child, riding a pony.

I'm following my father, but
he rides on, encircled with a
jewel-studded light, blinding
as a saber, or a cross.

"Wait Daddy!" I cry, "wait!"
As we ride past the cliff-faces
of white shale, the fossils close in, ammonite
and mollusk, rainbow shells, iridescent,
yet empty, old, damp, pristine shells; there's no light
left
to the colors. The sunlight disappears and it's
suddenly as
cold and damp as a mine shaft. "Wait!" Or a grave.

I have ridden 38 miles on my pony.
It's late, and I wonder where the gardenias have gone.
They're not gardenias (says a voice, his voice)
Not white petals. These are plumes

and fall with the drift of the angels.

But these plumes, I thought, were only fossils

feather fossils, touching me where the darkness had left.

Yet I remember, long ago, when the world was formed

from a single falling feather, I remember when the world

was young, younger than me, and worn like a plume

in an Easter hat, a shell in the crown, also white and pristine.

(same stanza)

unfettered, abundant, yet hopeful for more

seeds, more bounty, yet falling

as a bird shot from the sky,

& suddenly I know, *this is the key,*

falling, as a bird in the bodark shot,

with the drift of angels.

"… and tonight, as I stand before God, my salute shall sweep all the stars away from the blue threshold."

falling with the drift of the angels.

(April – May 1999)

[Editor's note: written after her diagnosis with multiple sclerosis]

ABOUT THE AUTHOR

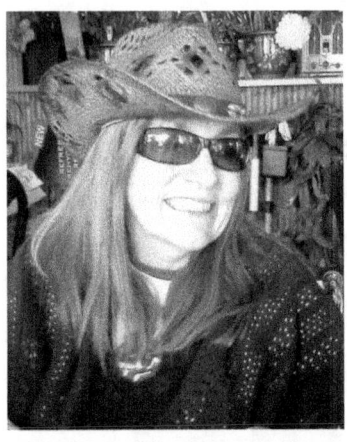

A poet, artist, writer, photographer and traveler,
Susan D. Baker produced a diverse and impressive body of
work, some of which is presented here. Her previous
published work includes a *Language Guide to French Polynesia*
(1996) and an edited volume of pen and ink drawings
entitled *The Whimsical Pen* (2006). Multiple sclerosis has
impacted her ability to create on the page, but she
continues to share her wry sense of humor and love of life
with others in Tucson, Arizona.